Hundreds
Easy & Practical
Mom-Tested
Activities
for **Kids**

Raising

Kids...

For the **fun** of it!

Wendy Johnson
Gloria McInnis
Heather Tansem

Published by *Raising Kids*
Printed in Canada by Friesens Corporation

National Library of Canada Cataloguing in Publication

Johnson, Wendy, 1958-
    Raising kids… for the fun of it! : hundreds of easy and practical mom-tested activities for kids / Wendy Johnson, Gloria McInnis, Heather Tansem.

Includes index.
ISBN 0-9734143-0-8

    1. Child rearing. 2. Creative activities and seat work.
I. McInnis, Gloria, 1961- II. Tansem, Heather, 1959- III. Title.

HQ755.8.J628 2004   649'.1   C2004-900570-7

To book a speaker or order additional copies, contact the authors at:

Raising Kids
P.O. Box 45087,
Lansdowne Postal Outlet,
Edmonton, Alberta,
Canada T6H 5Y1

Email: authors@raisingkids.ca

Website: **www.raisingkids.ca**

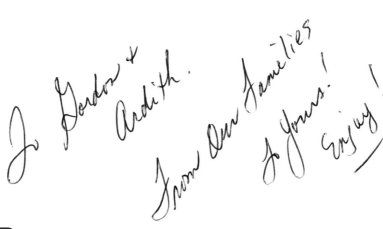

To Gordon & Ardith.
From Our Families
to Yours! Enjoy!

Dedication

We dedicate this book to our husbands and to our kids
*   to Glenn Johnson, Laura and Andrea,*
*   to Glenn McInnis, David and Matthew,*
*   and to Garry Tansem, Riley, Reid and Parker.*

Without you – we would not have begun this book.
Without your endless support – we could not have
completed it.

Our love and thanks to each one of you.

Acknowledgements

We want to acknowledge the people in our lives that have influenced the way we 'raise our kids'. Sharing stories and experiences, watching and listening to parents that we admire, through conversation, laughter and fun, we truly become better parents. We send thanks to our own parents, our relatives and our good friends—you have inspired us! Together we share this parenting journey.

Table of Contents ━━━━━━━━━━━━━

"Dads and Moms will find this 'tool kit' full of simple, fun activities that will enchant their children and keep them playful, safe and bonded to their family. Pick a page, roll up your sleeves and dive in for fun!"
Dr. Jim Canniff, Family Psychologist

Introduction

Good ideas can impact and literally transform your day. Moms are constantly getting ideas from one another that can make a difference in each other's lives and that is exactly what motivated us to write, **'Raising Kids...for the fun of it!'** It is a seasonal collection of great ideas and activities for your family. The ideas are simple, practical and best of all—they're 'Mom-tested'; every single one has been used in at least one of our families.   Concrete examples accompany many of these ideas and are marked with a star (★).

> ★ *"One summer day the kids were looking for something to do. We started pulling items out of the garage and from around the yard, and we set up an obstacle course. Just one activity kept us entertained and active for hours." (see p.162)*
>
> ★ *"I was pulling my hair out one evening because the kids just couldn't get settled into their homework—one was looking for an eraser and the other for some pencil crayons. Pretty soon they were fighting over the only ruler they could find. That was it, enough time wasted! We put together a homework basket so all the supplies would be in one handy location. One small idea has impacted how we do our homework every day." (see p.19)*
>
> ★ *"We were chatting around the fireplace with the kids one night and began sharing our most embarrassing moments. We were able to laugh about situations that were once quite upsetting. Dad started telling us about the time he asked a girl out and she refused him. It led to some very good lessons for our teenagers. One conversation starter set the tone for some great family interaction." (see p.132)*
>
> ★ *"One night everyone seemed a little 'off'. That evening for dinner I served dessert first and simply said, 'It's backwards day'. Such a simple little idea changed the atmosphere in our home instantly." (see p.135)*

The book is written in four seasonal sections and begins in the fall—as the new school year unfolds; so does the book. It's jam-packed with ideas, tips, strategies, step-by-step and how-to's—so basically, the planning is done for you. Use it as a resource book. As you manage your day-to-day issues, as you face parenting challenges or when you just need an activity or an idea—go to this book and find one.

This book is for parents with kids aged five to thirteen. However, we have learned through experience, that many of the ideas can be used or modified for almost any age, especially when they are done together as a family.

Our wish...is that these little nuggets will inspire you and ultimately, when you use them, make a positive difference in your family.

Book Categories

There are six different categories in the book, marked with icons for easy identification.

■ Family Fun

Build strong family bonds through laughter and play. Add zest to any ordinary day with cool ideas like puzzlemania, building a leprechaun trap or designing an obstacle course in your own back yard. Look for the 'Family Fun' icon to inject fun into any day!

■ Party Time

Create a great theme party. Be inspired by ingenious ideas for invitations, decorations, loot bags and step-by-step instructions for games and activities. Your kids will love to choose from a variety of parties like a detective party, slumber party or beach party. Search for this icon and find creative celebrations they'll never forget!

■ Family Discussions

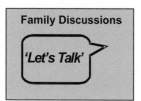

Connect with family members and build unity through discussion. Get your kids involved in conversation and decision-making on issues like allowances, how to deal with the unexpected or New Year's resolutions. Locate numerous topics for your family to explore with this icon. Is there anything your family needs to discuss…'Let's talk'.

■ Positive Parenting

Enrich your relationship with your children by being proactive and positive in how you approach parenting. Go on a 'date-night' with your child to show them how important they are, or support your child after a tough day by using active listening. The 'Positive Parenting' icon leads you to some new ideas for your 'parenting repertoire'.

■ Focus on Learning

The 'Focus on Learning' icon will help you access ideas ranging from effective study skills and homework routines to goal setting. Use these strategies to minimize homework tension and foster the home-school partnership.

■ Organized Living

Want to avoid feeling stressed out and wasting precious time? Organization is the key. Look for ideas on menu planning, creating a Christmas of your dreams and travel tips. In addition, there are numerous gift lists sure to solve any gift-giving dilemma. The 'organized living' icon directs you to ideas and plans to help create calm in your home.

"Inspired by love, these three Moms have set out to create an environment rich with activity and creative play. To understand the importance of intentional interaction is to accept the role of a purposeful parent."

Lori Runzer B.Sc.O.T.
'Strengthening Communities One Family at a Time'
Talk Show Host - CORUS Entertainment

"Finally, a parenting book with a totally fresh approach...a collection of the best of the best innovative and trusted ideas that make a house a home, promote family fun and build lasting connections.... a keeper! You'll want to use this book and pass it on to your kids when they become Moms and Dads."
Wendy Clarahan, Teacher, Professional Home Economist

Fall

Get Ready – Get Set – And Go !

It's 'Back to School' time. You can almost feel the excitement in the air as the kids anticipate the first day unfolding—who will my new teacher be? Who is in my class with me? For a parent, September can be one of the busiest and most stressful months of the year. Registration, early mornings, more structure, lunches and bus schedules are a big adjustment after a slower-paced summer vacation. Here are some tips and strategies for coping with September so you can Get Ready – Get Set – And Go!

Get Ready

■ Return to good routines and habits:

- During the week before the start of school get the kids to bed earlier and get them up earlier so the adjustment to the school schedule will be easier.
- Encourage your kids to brush up on some of their school skills by practising a few math facts and reading stories at bedtime.
- Prepare them for the inevitable questions about what they did during their summer vacation by reviewing all the highlights and activities with them. Rehearse how they will describe their holiday or encourage them to write about it in their journal.

■ Help your children prepare for the return to school:

- If your children will be taking a different bus than last year, show them where the bus stops for pickup and drop off.
- Pack their backpack with indoor shoes and enough school supplies for the first day. Don't load them down with everything on day one.

■ Get yourself organized:

- You'll receive newsletters, application forms, notices for sports try-outs and flyers. Designate a place in your kitchen where you can store a small file box or three ring binder. Label folders for each child's school information and for each type of activity they're involved in. Or make a separate section for each child in a binder. As the papers start coming through your door you're ready to:
  - write important dates on the family calendar
  - write and send cheques as soon as possible
  - file papers as soon as you've finished reading them
  - discard any unnecessary papers

> *Make extra copies of your child's birth certificate and health care cards so you are ready for sports registration.*

Get Set

■ On the first day back to school:

- Get up 20-30 minutes earlier than normal to avoid rushing. Keep calm and relaxed and your children will be calmer too.
- Discuss with your children what time they need to be home or at a designated meeting place.
- If you can't pick up the kids after school, then make alternate arrangements with them, like walking home with a friend.
- Arrange a special lunch – invite a friend over to share their excitement and to have a break from the school environment.
- If sending a lunch, be sure it doesn't require any special preparation. Microwaves or kettles aren't always available the first day of school.

> ★ *"Getting up 20 minutes earlier and being calm made a great start to a big day. What a contrast to last year when I was hollering at the kids to 'hurry up' because we were going to be late."* ★

> ★ *"We like to have some fun getting ready for the new school year. There are school supplies to buy, clothes to choose and new shoes to purchase. I like to plan a lunch or dinner together and do our shopping one-on-one with each of my kids. We treat it like a special event and make a date to shop for the new school year."* ★

And Go

■ Discuss the first day of school over dinner:

Talk about your child's new classmates, teacher and what happened throughout the day.
- *What's your teacher's name?*
- *How many different teachers do you have?*
- *Which friends are in your class?*
- *Who are you sitting next to?*
- *Who did you play with at recess?*

■ Establish homework routines from 'Day One':

As soon as homework is assigned, have your children complete it. Stay on top of assignments right from the start of the year. Get started on the home reading program, spelling lists and math facts as soon as the teacher sends home the information.

Raising Kids…for the fun of it!

■ Focus on healthy habits:

Many children miss school during the first few weeks back due to some bug they have picked up at school. Here are some suggestions to keep your family healthy:

- Take a daily multi-vitamin.
- Remind your children to wash their hands before lunch at school and again when they come home after school.
- Make healthy, nutritious food to help their bodies cope with the change in schedule and additional stress.
- Get enough sleep – adequate sleep benefits the immune system and helps them focus at school.
- Include activity in their daily routine – especially after sitting at a desk all day they need physical activity.

■ Plan to:

- Attend 'Meet the Teacher' night – start to develop rapport with your child's teacher and start the school year off on the right foot.
- Attend the School Council meeting – get the *inside scoop* about decisions that affect your child's school.
- Go to the registration for out-of-school activities like dance, music and sports.
- Shop for unexpected school supplies.
- Spend extra time with your children while they adjust to their new routine.

Benefits of attending 'Meet the Teacher Night':
- *Learn about the teacher's philosophy and expectations.*
- *Get the advantage of hearing first-hand information about the upcoming year and receive important material.*
- *Build rapport with the teacher that will help you to be a partner in your child's education.*
- *Give your child the message that their school is important to you.*

★ *"My son burst through the door after school one afternoon. Clenched in his hand was the agenda for 'Meet the Teacher Night'. He told me how he had organized his desk and laid out some scribblers for me to review. He was so excited that I was meeting his teacher tonight. I decided right then that I would have to postpone my shopping trip until later in the week. I had a meeting with the teacher that I couldn't miss."* ★

Homework Tips

Your expectations and approach to homework will set the tone for your children's learning at home. Establish good homework habits early. Organization and structure are key elements to making homework time more productive, effective and enjoyable. Use these homework guidelines:

1. **Let your children know what your expectations are.** Be clear with your children that you expect them to do quality work at home as well as in school.

2. **Get your child a study planner or assignment book.** Encourage them to get into the habit of writing down their assignments and checking them off when they are completed.

3. **Establish a routine.** Decide when and where homework is to be done.

4. **Set up a study area for each child.** Provide a quiet, comfortable, well-lit place for studying, complete with pens, pencils, erasers, paper and other school supplies.

5. **Suggest that your child work on tough subjects first.** They will have more energy at the beginning of their homework period and therefore will be better able to tackle a harder assignment.

6. **Help your child**. Let them know that you are ready to help with any areas that they find difficult or that frustrates them.

7. **Begin working on assignments early.** Encourage your child to work on an assignment as soon as it is given to avoid a backlog and cramming.

8. **Lengthy projects need a plan.** Help your child to start with an outline of all the things that need to be done and when they need to be completed. Include the beginning phase of research, drafting, editing and then through to final copy. Review your child's progress and help revise the schedule as necessary.

9. **Teach your child good exam study habits.** If an exam is coming up, get them to study daily for 20-30 minutes to avoid last minute cramming. Help your child by testing them on the information they've studied. Encourage your child to review areas of difficulty by going over their notes. Have your children make up their own sample test questions; by going through their study materials and creating 'fill in the blank' or 'mix and match' questions.

Raising Kids…for the fun of it!

10. **Keep open communication with your child's teachers and the school.** E-mail is an easy and efficient way to keep in touch.

11. **Limit screen time!** Allow television, computers or video games after all homework is completed.

12. **Encourage physical activity.** If your child is working on homework for a long period of time, take them out for a brisk 20 minute walk or bike ride in the fresh air to help them get some exercise and be able to refocus. Physical activity is important every day, especially after long hours of sitting at school.

13. **Offer a reward for good effort.** We would all like our children to do well in school and get high marks. But high academic achievement is unrealistic for many children and instead of focusing on the mark your child achieves, focus on the effort they put into their work. Encourage and congratulate them for their best effort regardless of the mark they receive.

★ *"Between the relaxed pace of summer holidays still fresh in our minds and the fabulous fall weather, we found it difficult to get back into school routines of homework and studying in September. It was tough, but our perseverance paid off when the kids came home with their first report card. They had a great start to their academic year. This was such a difference from the prior year when we let things slide a bit through September."* ★

Dealing with the Unexpected

Early in September, have a family meeting to discuss after-school routines and how you'll handle delays or unexpected situations. If you normally pick up your child from school, what should they do if you are late? Kids are often upset and unprepared when arrangements are changed at the last minute. Develop a plan with your child so they will know what to do. A plan will give them peace of mind and confidence to face the unexpected.

■ Discussion Topics

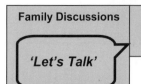

- Where and when you'll meet your child after school.
- What they should do if you don't arrive at the designated spot by a certain time or when most of the other children have gone home.
- If you could, how you would notify them if you are going to be late.
- What they should do if they miss their bus.
- Talk to your child about who they need to call in case of an emergency if they can't reach you. Write out your cell phone number, work number and a neighbour or friend's number in their agenda book or onto a card for your child's backpack.
- If they take public transit make sure they have coins in a small compartment of their backpack to make phone calls, or for bus fare if they have misplaced their bus pass.

> ★ *"One winter day when my daughter was in grade two, I was held up in traffic on my way to pick her up from school. I arrived at the school 20 minutes late. There she was standing in the cold and crying, just a few feet from the front doors of the school. I felt horrible. That night we came up with a plan for what she should do if I was delayed again. We decided she would wait inside the school doors, and watch for me from the window. That way I could call the school and I'd know where they could find her. Equipped with a plan, she felt more confident and prepared if it happened again."* ★

Homework Supplies

Do you find your children wasting valuable study time looking for a pencil, eraser, scissors or markers? Gather school supplies left over from last year, add other supplies they'll need and put them all in one convenient place at home – a 'homework basket'.

■ Homework Basket Contents

pencils	scissors	tape
pencil sharpener	glue sticks	loose leaf paper
pens	white glue	plain paper
erasers	ruler	paper clips
fine markers	calculator	reinforcements
wide markers	scrap pad	white-out
pencil crayons		stapler

After School Activities

There are so many great programs and activities available to children, the selection seems endless. But many parents and child-rearing experts are recommending we resist the temptation to enrol in too many activities, filling our child's schedule. Be sure you have enough down time for your family and leave time for your child to 'just be a kid'.

★ *"My oldest daughter is a social creature. She loves school, scheduled activities after school and lots of play dates. My younger daughter needs some solitude and time away from everyone after school. I've learned over the years to honour their different personalities and to respond to their individual needs. There are so many interesting and fun activities available for kids these days; it is hard to resist signing up for more. But just because I **can** fit more into the family schedule, doesn't mean I **should**. I've learned to be sensitive to each of my child's needs — they're happier for it and so am I."* ★

Supporting Your Child After a Tough Day

It is inevitable that your child will be upset at some time about some thing at school. Perhaps they were teased at recess, were not included in a game, they annoyed their teacher or did poorly on an exam. Here are some strategies for helping them to cope with difficulties and to teach them how to deal with their problems:

- First, be a good listener – help your child describe how they are feeling without being judgmental and try not to minimize their feelings.
- Let them 'get it all out', use words like *umm* and *uh-huh,* or *I see,* to encourage them to keep talking so that you hear the whole story.
- Don't immediately jump in with a solution.
- Show empathy – imagine how you would feel in their shoes at their age.
- Share your ideas with them; relate some experience from your past.
- Help them find solutions, discuss options and role-play to demonstrate some language they might use if they are ever faced with a similar situation.
- Spend some one-on-one time with them; bake cookies, read a book or play a game of cards.
- Get some exercise together; take a walk, shoot some hoops or play catch.

> ★ *"One day my child seemed very frustrated after school. When I asked him questions about his day, he didn't offer any information that would help me understand why he was upset. I suggested we go for a walk. Eventually we reached the banks of the ravine and there we sat down. As we looked across the riverbank and starting chatting, the stories started to flow. I found out about a few things that had been bothering him. It was a great release. After awhile we got up and headed home. We decided we wouldn't tell the rest of the family exactly where we had been and we'd keep the place on the banks of the ravine as 'our secret spot'. We've returned to that spot many times since. It is always a safe place to think out loud, to talk about our feelings or sometimes just to vent."* ★

Classroom Help From Home

After the first month when everyone is settled into the school routine, your child's teacher may ask for volunteers. Many parents want to volunteer to help in their child's classroom but are not able to because of work commitments or because they have younger children at home. Talk with your child's teacher about the kind of support they need or suggest some of these ideas for making a valued contribution.

- Help with a spelling program where you review student journals weekly and write a personalized list of misspelled words.
- Craft preparation – cut out shapes or do other preparation that will make things go more smoothly during class time.
- Sewing projects – sew painting smocks or other projects.
- Mail order book club – compile the order and select free books for the class.
- Call parents to organize food and decorations for the class party.

★ *"When I went back to work after my second child started grade one I felt so disconnected from his life. I was used to being in the classroom once a week helping with the reading program. Unfortunately, my schedule no longer allowed that freedom. I talked with his teacher and she suggested I help out by calling a few other moms to organize the Halloween party. I was so glad I could be included, even though I couldn't be in the classroom."* ★

Organized Living

Menu Planning

How much time and energy do you spend every day fretting about what to make for supper? Are you tired of running to the grocery store or stopping on the way home for one or two missing ingredients? Try planning ahead for just one week of meals and see if menu planning makes a difference for you. Here are some suggestions to get you started.

1. **Ask your family what they like to eat and make a list of meal ideas.** To increase the variety:
   - Ask your friends what their family favourites are.
   - Review your cookbooks for recipes you would like to make.

2. **Get out the calendar and review your time commitments.** Pick meals that work with your schedule.
   - Choose a slow cooker recipe when you have time early in the day.
   - Plan for leftovers or make meals that are quick to prepare on days when you have little time just before supper.

> ★ *"I just couldn't get through the busy fall without menu planning. There are so many benefits. My family eats more healthy meals, we are less tempted to run out to a restaurant and we are saving money by having the groceries purchased in advance. The kids love the variety and looking at the schedule to see what's coming. This was one of the best organizational tips I ever tried!"* ★

3. **Decide which meals to serve for the next week and write them down in your day timer or on the family calendar.**

4. **Make a grocery list of the ingredients you need to buy for the week's meals.**

5. **Do the grocery shopping.**

6. **Complete as many of the 'make ahead steps' as possible on the weekend.** Sauté several pounds of ground beef and then divide it into portions for sloppy joes, spaghetti sauce, tacos, hamburger soup and freeze.

7. **Stick to your plan.** Rest assured you have the necessary ingredients on hand for tonight's meal.

> *Wash all fruit and cut vegetables so they are ready to eat for a quick healthy snack or to add to a meal, soup or stew.*

Menu Plan for a Week – Here's a Sample

Sunday	Monday	Tuesday	Wednesday	Thursday	Friday	Saturday
chicken and pasta	tacos	meat pie	barbecued salmon	lasagne	pork roast	hamburger soup

Groceries:
salmon
chicken breasts
3 lbs. hamburger
frozen lasagne
meat pies   pork roast
taco kit
lemon   tomatoes
carrots   broccoli
potatoes   rice
parsley   2 bags salad
milk   yogurt
cheese   eggs

★ *"Menu planning worked so well for me that now I menu plan for the whole month at a time. I still do a weekly shopping trip to get my ingredients, but only have to create a plan once a month. It is such a time saver."* ★

Thanksgiving – a Time for Gratitude

Thanksgiving is the time of year to reflect on your good fortune and to be thankful for what you have. Whatever you do to celebrate, be sure to take a few moments to savour the season of gratitude. Ask your children to draw a picture, write a letter or discuss the things in their lives for which they are thankful.

★ *"This year we received a handmade Thanksgiving card from our neighbours. I was so touched by the message they wrote 'Our family is thankful for your friendship'. We especially appreciated the sentiment at Thanksgiving."* ★

Thanksgiving Place Cards

Need an activity to keep the kids busy while you prepare dinner? Let the kids help 'set the scene' by creating personalized place cards for family members and guests. Cut white card stock into 2" x 4" (5 cm x 10 cm) and fold them in half lengthwise. This will allow the place cards to stand up in front of the dinner plates. Gather felt pens, Thanksgiving stickers, stamps, leaves and berries for the young artists to add some flair to the dinner table.

Enjoy Thanksgiving Dinner

Enjoy each other's company after the big meal. Encourage your children to stay at the table and be part of the after-dinner conversation. Try some of these games and conversation starters while still seated around the table.

- **Play 'I Spy'** – a great game to include young children. The original game is where you look for something of a certain colour, e.g. *I spy something that is red, what is it?* Go around the table allowing each person to make a guess. Modify the game so that you are looking for something that starts with a specific letter, e.g. *I spy something that starts with the letter 'm' what is it?* Let each person guess a word such as *Mom* or *milk*.

- **Collectively tell a story** – have each person contribute one word at a time. Start with the youngest child who says a word to begin the story such as '*Once*', then the person next to them says a word '*upon*', then the next adds '*a*' and so on. After a few times around the table the story can be quite hilarious. For a variation try saying two words at a time, like '*Sheila left*', the next person might add '*her shoe*' and so on.

> ★ *"During Thanksgiving dinner this year, our guests led us in a beautiful family prayer:*
> *For food - in a world where many walk in hunger,*
> *For friends - in a world where many walk alone,*
> *For faith - in a world where many walk in fear,*
> *We give you thanks, Oh God."* ★

- **Be 'in the spotlight'** – let one person at a time be the centre of attention. Everyone else tries to guess their favourite colour, sport, meal, dessert, TV show, movie, vacation spot, music group and so on. Give each family member a turn in the spotlight.

- **Share your gratitude** – ask each person to say something they are especially thankful or grateful for.

> ★ *"We encourage our kids to stay at the table and visit after a big family meal. When they were young we started playing word games and 'I Spy' to include them in an activity that would hold their attention. Now at Thanksgiving we take turns saying things that we are especially grateful for. We have found that after we go around the table once and hear each other's ideas, it prompts more. The kids are excited to add other things they are thankful for and want to go around the table again."* ★

Enjoy the Fall Season

Before the fall season slips by and turns into winter, take time to relish the season and spend some time outdoors.

■ Enjoy the Season

- Take a walk and enjoy the magnificent fall colours.
- Feed the birds in a ravine or park.
- Collect leaves, pine cones, berries, twigs, feathers and stones to create a collage, picture frame, wreath or table centerpiece.
- Go to the pumpkin patch or corn maze.

■ Have Some Group Fun

- Play road hockey with those old hockey sticks or even a broom handle.
- Play bocce ball, croquet or football.

■ Try Some Sidewalk Chalk Games

King's Court

Number of players: 4
Setup:
- Draw a large square 6 m by 6 m (or smaller if space is limited) and draw two diagonal lines to divide it into 4 equal parts.
- Draw a 1 meter square in the center of the large square.

Object of the game: To have the fewest points.
Play: Each player is assigned a side and stands outside the large square. Choose one person to begin the game. They pass the ball to any of the other three players, but it must first bounce in the center square. The receiving player catches it after one bounce and then bounce passes it to any of the other three players without leaving the spot where he caught it. If a receiver is unable to catch the bounce pass, he gets a point. If the passer bounces the ball outside of the center square, he gets a point. The winner is the player with the fewest points.

★ *"Often in the fall our family walks to the neighbourhood park taking along the camera and tripod. After scouting out the best background of colourful leaves and grasses, we take some candid and posed shots of the family. The fall landscape is so beautiful captured in a photo. I have copies made of the best picture, and they are ready to slip in with our Christmas cards."* ★

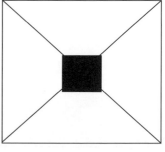

Outdoor Halloween Decorations

Set the scene and have some fun this Halloween. Try these ideas for outdoor decorations that will surely set your house apart from the others on the street. Enjoy the spirit of Halloween and even dress up to surprise the trick or treaters that come-a-knocking.

Stuffed Animal Display

Here's a unique approach to Halloween decorating that youngsters will enjoy—find your favourite stuffed animals and dress them up in simple Halloween costumes. Create a display on your front step, front window or foyer.

What you'll need:
- a variety of sizes and types of stuffed animals
- dress-up hats, glasses, accessories and jewellery
- infant-sized clothing or small pieces of fabric wrapped around and pinned to the stuffed animals (e.g. use polka-dotted or striped fabric for a clown costume)
- plastic spiders, bats, bugs, pumpkins
- old Halloween masks and props
- table or chairs
- boxes
- large dark sheet or tablecloth

★ *"When my children were young we set up a display in our front window every Halloween. It included several stuffed animals dressed in costume, such as a bear dressed as a pirate, a stuffed dog dressed as a clown, and Winnie the Pooh dressed as Little Red Riding Hood. The kids loved creating the display, and on Halloween night many adults and young children have stood at our window to admire our very scary stuffies."* ★

Disguise the stuffed animals:
- **Dr. Bear** – a big teddy bear dressed as a doctor in green fabric with a white mask and toy stethoscope around his neck.
- **Sheriff Dog** – a big stuffed dog dressed in a cowboy hat, bandanna and sheriff's badge.
- **Princess Bear** – a small bear dressed as a princess in a tiara, necklace and some shiny fabric draped around her body.
- **Witch Rabbit** – a rabbit dressed as a witch, in a black wig and pointed black hat. Place a small stuffed cat next to her.

To set up the display:

Place one or two tables or chairs in your display area. To facilitate several levels on the table, add boxes of varying heights and then cover with a large sheet or tablecloth. Place 'dressed up' stuffed animals on the different levels and add a variety of Halloween decorations like plastic spiders, bugs or small pumpkins. Illuminate the display with a spotlight and shut off the other lights in the room or entrance.

SomeBODY is Trapped Under the Garage Door!

Have some fun this Halloween creating the illusion that a person is trapped under the garage door.

What you'll need:
- old pair of jeans
- crumpled newspaper
- boots
- spooky music or scary sounds
- portable CD player

■ Here's how to create your scene:

Stuff an old pair of jeans with crumpled newspaper and position boots at the end of the pants, as if they are being worn. Lay the pants on the ground and close the overhead garage door overtop of the waistband of the pants. Turn off the lights and play spooky music or creepy sounds from your garage. It's sure to entertain your trick or treaters!

> ★ *"I'm not sure who had more fun; my husband, creating the scary scene, or the kids taken by surprise as they walked past the garage. After setting up the spooky music and dry ice, Glenn stuffed and arranged the clothing to make it look like someone was lying partly into the garage and partly on the driveway. Then he lowered the garage door so it just rested on the trapped body. He chuckled all evening as the kids commented when they came to the door for treats."* ★

Raising Kids…for the fun of it!

Create Peter Pumpkin Head

This type of scarecrow looks great propped up in a lawn chair by your front door. He's a terrific addition to any outdoor Halloween display. And he'll surely be talked about as he surprises your unsuspecting guests.

What you'll need:
- 24" (60 cm) garden stake
- 16" (40 cm) garden stake
- 2" (5cm) nail and hammer
- dark colored old clothes (shirt or coat, pants, boots, gloves, scarf and hat)
- newspaper
- lawn chair with a high back
- a 'head-sized' pumpkin
- black permanent felt marker
- 2 safety pins

★ *"It was hilarious to watch. People thought our Peter Pumpkin Head was a live person sitting in the chair by our front door. It took their breath away. He was so popular, the following Halloween he began sprouting up all over the neighbourhood."* ★

Here's how to create 'Peter Pumpkin Head':

1. **Make the frame.**
   - Nail the two stakes together in the shape of a cross; connect the 16" (40 cm) stake about 6" (15 cm) from the top of the 24" (60 cm) stake. The horizontal stake creates the shoulders; the vertical stake creates the spine.

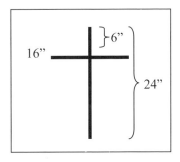

2. **Create Peter's body propped in a chair.**
   - Stuff a pair of pants with wads of crumpled newspaper and seat them in the chair.
   - Place the stake inside the pants and lean it on the back of the chair. Position the chair against a wall for added support.
   - Stuff the shirt or jacket and button it up over top of the horizontal stake.
   - Put the legs into the boots and pin on the gloves at the end of the sleeves.

3. **Create his head.**
   - Carve a hole in the bottom of the pumpkin, slightly smaller than the vertical stake. Push the pumpkin down onto the stake until it rests on the shoulders.

4. **Add the finishing touches.**
   - Use a black marker to draw a jack-o-lantern face; be sure to include a furrowed brow or crow's feet around his eyes.
   - Cover the neck with a scarf and put a hat on the top of Peter's head.

Have Some Pumpkin Fun

Eat supper under the glow of the jack-o-lantern. *Put your pumpkin in the centre of the table, light the candle, turn off the kitchen lights and dine by the light of the jack-o-lantern.*

Too young to carve a pumpkin? *Create jack-o-lanterns by using black markers to draw a face on the pumpkin. Or create a paper mache pumpkin that you keep and display year after year.*

Elegant pumpkins. *Spray paint pumpkins with metallic gold or bronze paint to create unusual, but beautiful decorations. Arrange them on your front step and they will almost 'glow' in the dark.*

Raising Kids…for the fun of it!

The 'Halloween Spirit'

Try this spooky little gag on your friends. Go to the dollar store to buy enough treats and inexpensive decorations to fill three Halloween bags. Have fun knocking on doors and secretly leaving behind a bag, along with the Spirit's note, for your friends to enjoy. The idea here is that each friend will also make three Halloween bags filled with goodies to give to their friends and so on. Enjoy the little secret as Halloween excitement spreads throughout your neighbourhood.

★ *"A couple of weeks before Halloween our doorbell rang. When the girls opened the door there was no one in sight. They were, however, delighted to find a bag of treats and the Spirit's letter. They couldn't wait to play this prank on their friends. We prepared three bags and set out to deliver them. We rang the doorbell and quickly hid behind a tree. Our hearts were thumping as we hoped they hadn't seen us make the delivery. By the end of the week everyone in the neighbourhood was talking about the Halloween Spirit."* ★

*The 'Spirit of the Season'
is with you now 'til Halloween.
He was delivered by someone,
who hopefully was not seen.*

*A friend has selected you,
to receive a lovely treat.
They hope you do enjoy it,
and think it's really neat!*

*Now put the Spirit's picture,
by your door for all to see.
That you've already had a visit,
and received it gleefully.*

*Then pack 3 bags of goodies,
like the one that you just got.
Ring a friend's bell and leave their loot,
make sure you don't get caught!*

*Remember to include this poem,
and the Spirit's picture too.
Spread some fun 'round your neighbourhood.
Happy Halloween to you!*

Family Fun

Halloween Costumes

It is so much fun to dress up in costume for Halloween. Kids and adults alike enjoy pretending to be someone or something else. Besides the obvious costumes at department stores, where do you look for great Halloween costumes?

Where to Look for Halloween Costume Ideas

- Go to the fabric store and look through the pattern books.
- Look through magazines.
- Check out your kid's tickle trunk for costume pieces.
- Look at costume rental or retail stores.
- Check out the thrift shop or second-hand stores.
- Exchange costumes with friends or neighbours.
- Check out the latest movies or cartoon characters.
- Write down the best costumes you saw this year to give you ideas and inspiration for next year.

Try Creating Simple Costumes

Spider – Stuff three pairs of black nylons with fibrefill and attach them to the back of a black t-shirt. Wear black pants or leggings and a black t-shirt. You might want to apply black makeup to your face, or wear large dark sunglasses.

A Table – Cut a hole in the top of a large box, slip it over your head and slide it down to your waist. Add a tablecloth and glue on some paper plates, cutlery and cups.

Mummy – Wind yourself up in 3" strips of white fabric or sheets. Use white athletic tape as needed to hold strips in place.

Ms. Frizzle – Carry a cardboard bus (similar to Magic School Bus), put on a flowery dress, frizz your hair and add glasses.

Mad Scientist – White lab coat, big dark rimmed glasses and nose, black curly haired wig, tie, toy stethoscope, fake blood.

Queen/Princess/Fairy – For the Princess, modify an old elegant lacy dress, add a tiara and fancy shoes. Just add wings to create a Fairy.

Waldo – Red striped t-shirt, dark-rimmed glasses and hat.

Raising Kids…for the fun of it!

Shepherd – Striped housecoat, one medium sized towel on your head with one rolled towel or scarf wrapped around head to secure it. Carry a long cane or shepherd's staff.

Cowboy – Sheriff's badge, bandanna, jeans and cowboy hat.

Surgeon – Green clothes, toy stethoscope and blood pressure band.

A boy dressed as a woman – A boy can wear one of his Mom's dresses and stuff balloons in the bodice, or wear her housecoat with rollers in his hair.

A girl dressed as a man – A girl can wear a suit and tie and carry a briefcase.

Reindeer – Dress in brown clothing, put on reindeer antlers (from your Christmas decorations), paint a red circle on your nose.

Football player – Wear a jersey and helmet and black makeup under eyes.

Arthur – Try a golden yellow long-sleeved shirt, black rimmed round glasses.

Harry Potter – Round glasses, white shirt, tie, crested sweater and pin a stuffed owl to your shoulder.

Grandma and Grandpa – pair up with a friend, add some padding to a dress and apron for Grandma. Get a pair of trouser with suspenders and a cardigan for Grandpa. Top it off with glasses and add some baby powder to your hair to color it grey.

> ★ *"My neighbour is so resourceful. She can make a costume out of nearly anything. The Halloween her daughter was a spider was so neat! Just a few pairs of black pantyhose, black makeup and she was ready."* ★

Kids love Halloween; the costumes, treats and the uneasy spooky atmosphere. Host a house party or use these ideas to create a school party with lots of fun centres.

Skeleton Invitation

What you'll need:
- black card stock
- white paper
- black marker
- scissors
- tape
- glue
- copies of skeleton head and torso
- 8 silver paper clips per invitation
- white gel pen

How to create the skeleton invitation:
1. Trace or photocopy a skeleton head and torso; cut one out for each invitation.
2. Cut or fold the black card stock into cards.
3. Using 8 paper clips per invitation, link the paper clips together in sets of two; they become the skeleton's arms and legs.
4. Tape the arms and legs on the construction paper while you temporarily position the torso over the paperclip limbs.

COME IF YOU DARE TO OUR
HALLOWEEN HOWLER
WEAR YOUR COSTUME AND BE READY
FOR A
FRIGHTFULLY GOOD TIME!
OCT 28TH
7PM TO 9PM
JANE'S HOUSE
RSVP TO THE WITCH 555-5679

5. Glue the skeleton head and torso onto the limbs, covering the tape.
6. Using a white gel pen, draw a word bubble coming from the skeleton's mouth with the words 'Come to our Halloween Howler'.
7. Write your own party details inside the card.

Decorations 'To Die For'

Use these cute Halloween jokes as party decorations. Cut out pumpkin or bat shapes and use chalk or white-out to write these jokes onto large sheets of orange or black paper. Hang them on the outside of your front door or on classroom walls. They can be laminated and used year after year.

 What do you call a ghost's mistake?
　　　...a boo-boo

 How do you make a tissue dance?
　　　...put a little bogey in it

 Knock, knock. Who's there? Philip...Philip who?
　　　...Philip my bag with candy please

 Which fairy tale do ghosts like best?
　　　...sleeping boo-ty

 What kind of horses do ghost kids like to ride?
　　　...night-mares

 What room in the house is a mummy afraid of?
　　　...the living room

What games do baby ghosts like to play?
　　　...peek-a-BOO

 Why don't monsters play hide-and-seek?
　　　...who'd look for them?

 What room in the house do ghosts really like?
　　　...the die-ning room

What do you get when you cross Dracula and Sleeping Beauty?
　　　...tired blood

 Why didn't the skeleton go to the party?
　　　...he didn't have no-body to go with

> ★ *"We tape up the laminated jokes each year for the younger kids to enjoy. We love to hear the giggles as the kids read the jokes on their way past our garage."* ★

What game do ghosts like best?
...hide & shriek

Ghoulish Garnish

■ For Your Drinks:

- **Add a floating frozen hand to your punch bowl.**
  1. Wash a latex glove.
  2. Dilute grenadine syrup with water and pour into the glove.
  3. Add vines from grapes for veins in the hand.
  4. Tie the wrist of the latex glove and freeze.
  5. Be cautious when removing the glove so you don't break off 'fingers'. Or you can cut off the glove from the frozen hand, rather than pulling it off.

- **Create swamp water or boo-berry drink.**
  1. Mix 2 kinds of juice or pop.
  2. When serving, add the slugs (gummy worms).

> **Add some atmosphere** to your Halloween party with dry ice. Be careful that no one touches it; the severely low temperature can burn skin.

■ For Your Vegetable Tray:

- **Add eyeballs.**
  1. Cut away most of the red skin from a few radishes.
  2. Core a 'plug' out of the middle of the radish.
  3. Insert a slice of a green olive to represent the iris.

- **Add a severed hand.**
  1. Spray the inside of a plastic glove with vegetable oil.
  2. Prepare Jello as instructions indicate, but use only half the amount of water to make a firmer 'jelly'.
  3. Pour the Jello into the latex glove, use a twist tie to close the opening and store in the fridge to 'set' the Jello.
  4. Once set, cut the glove from the hand and place it on a serving tray as garnish.

- **Add gummy worms or other candies to the tray.**

> ★ *"My daughter's classmates giggled and poked at the fake hand I included on the vegetable tray. It was such a 'scary' addition to their Halloween theme."* ★

Raising Kids...for the fun of it!

Simple But Effective Treats

■ Halloween Popcorn Cake

Melt 40 large marshmallows with ¼ cup (125 ml) margarine in a microwave safe bowl. Stir in 1 teaspoon (5 ml) vanilla. Coat 10 cups (2.5 l) of popped corn with the marshmallow mixture. Stir in 2 cups (500ml) of orange and black jujubes. Press firmly into a greased bundt pan or angel food pan. Let cool and set. Remove from pan and slice to serve.

■ Quick Spider Web Cake

With a little icing, turn an ordinary cake into a spider's web.
- 9" round cake
- chocolate icing to cover
- white icing for the web
- plastic spiders

Ice the entire cake with chocolate icing. Then use white icing to draw a solid circle in the center of the cake about the size of a quarter. Next, draw 3 or 4 circles around the centre circle, each about an inch apart. While icing is still pliable, pull the dull end of a knife from the centre of the white icing, through the circles to the outer edge of the cake to make the web. Place plastic spiders on top of the cake to complete the design.

■ Rice Krispie Pumpkins

Use your favourite Rice Krispie squares recipe and add a few drops of orange food colouring to the melted marshmallows. Press the mixture onto a large cookie sheet, creating a thin layer of rice krispie mixture; adjust thickness according to the height of your cookie cutter. Use a pumpkin-shaped cookie cutter to cut out the shapes. Spread a little green icing at the top of each one for a stem. Mark the eyes, nose and mouth with black icing.

★ *"I had so much fun putting on the class Halloween party. I asked around for activity ideas and created some of my own. The kids had a blast and I've used many of these ideas for several parties year after year."* ★

Party Activities

The following games are designed to work well as centres. You can divide children into groups of 4-6, or some of the activities are suitable for one large group. Some activities are quite lively and others can be used when you need to calm things down a bit. Centres 1 to 6 are for smaller groups, whereas centres 7 and 8 are suitable for a larger group.

■ Centre 1 – Guess My Picture

Write a number of Halloween-related words on pieces of paper and place them in a plastic pumpkin. Divide the players into 2 teams and give them a few minutes to pick their team name, perhaps 'Witches' vs 'Warlocks'. A player on the first team begins by picking out a slip of paper; he reads the word and keeps it privately to himself. Then he draws a picture of the word on a whiteboard, a blackboard or on a large pad of paper clipped onto an easel. Only the members of his team can guess what has been drawn. They have a maximum of 30 seconds or 1 minute (whatever you choose) to guess the picture. Use a timer to keep track. If the team guesses correctly, they get a point. Then it is the opposing team's turn. The team with the most points wins.

Try some of these easy words to begin with:

MOON   WITCH
PUMPKIN   KNIFE
GHOST   WART
BAT   BROOM

Here's some that are more challenging:

BLOOD   BLACK CAT
CANDY   CAULDRON
SKELETON   WITCH'S BREW
DRACULA   WARLOCK
HAUNTED HOUSE

★ *"We tried a variation where one member from each team came forward to look at the word. On the signal 'go', they both began drawing. The first team that guessed the correct word was awarded a point. When we had a tie, both teams got a point. Be prepared though; this variation can be much noisier! Everyone who walked by the classroom just had to peak in."* ★

Raising Kids…for the fun of it!

■ Centre 2 – Pin the Wart on the Witch

Play a variation of Pin the Tail on the Donkey by sticking the Wart on the Witch's Face, or Stick the Fang on Dracula's Mouth. For a bit more of a challenge, stick the Eyes on the Jack-O-Lantern.

■ Centre 3 – Pass the Pumpkin

Using a permanent black marker, draw a pumpkin face on two large oranges. Divide the group into two teams of equal number and have them line up in two rows. The first person in each row tucks the orange under their chin. On the signal 'go', they must pass it to the next person in line. Team members take a turn passing the orange from under their chin to the neck of their teammate who quickly passes it to the next person in line. The rule is that you cannot use your hands. If the orange falls at any point, it goes back to the beginning of the line. The winning team is the one that's first to get the orange securely under the chin of the person at the end of their line.

★ *"We played this relay many times—the kids just loved it!"* ★

■ Centre 4 – Create a Halloween Mural

Tape a long strip of white paper to a wall in the hall or classroom. Supply felt markers and have the kids take turns creating a huge Halloween mural. To help get the artistic juices flowing, paste or draw a few sample pictures like a creepy cat, haunted house, gnarly tree, bat, witch or Dracula on the mural. Party supply stores sell rolls of wide white paper (normally used as table cloths) that are perfect for this project! Or you can purchase rolls of paper at the craft store.

■ Centre 5 – The Cave of Darkness

★ *"My daughter's fondest Halloween memory was when she was in grade four and I created the 'Cave of Darkness' for her class. I blacked out the reading corner in her classroom the day before the party and taped the opening shut with harsh signs warning prospective trespassers to 'Keep Out or Be Cursed'. Just before the party, I stocked the tables with my gross concoctions and lit a couple of candles inside the cave to add to the spooky atmosphere. I dressed myself up as a sorcerer and practiced my story in my best scary voice. The kids came through the cave in small groups and listened intently. Some were too frightened to even feel the 'eyes' and 'intestines', until I whispered in their ear who I really was and that it was actually just soggy oatmeal. Many teachers came through the cave and several other classrooms of kids joined in. The 'Cave of Darkness' was a huge success. It was a fair amount of set up and preparation, but it was so worth it. We still talk about that Halloween."* ★

Create a spooky cave in the classroom and let their imaginations run away with them.

1. First, darken a corner of a classroom or small room by covering the windows with sheets of black paper or dark plastic garbage bags.

2. Prepare several ghastly concoctions ahead of time that will represent body parts and store them in separate ice-cream pails until the party. Your collection of brains, ears, eyes and intestines will appeal to the daring partygoers.

   A sampling of mock body parts include:
   - **Brains** – oatmeal porridge with only half of the water the recipe requires
   - **Intestines** – gummy worms or shoe string licorice soaked in oil
   - **Eyeballs** – peeled grapes
   - **Stomach contents** – marshmallows in oil
   - **Fingers** – wieners with wooden screws threaded lengthwise so it feels like there's a bone inside
   - **Kidney** – cook, drain and cool some pasta, leave it in a lump and add vegetable oil
   - **Appendix** – canned lychee nuts
   - **Liver** – pudding packed into a plastic bag, with a bit of pudding smeared on the outside of the bag

   Have a container of hand wipes available after this activity for the kids to clean-up.

Raising Kids…for the fun of it!

3. On a table inside the cave, arrange the pails of body parts.

4. Cover the pails with several large black garbage bags. Cut a slit in the plastic above each concoction so kids can slide their hand through the slit and into the pail to *feel* the contents but not *see* them.

5. Dress up as a witch or sorcerer and invite a few kids at a time into the Cave of Darkness. Tell some story about needing extra body parts to complete your gruesome recipe or experiment. Try this story for older children or make up your own version.

The Witch's Tale

"Long ago, near the swamp at the edge of town, lived an evil witch. She was often seen wandering the area, looking for something. Many years after her death, a diary was discovered describing her favourite pastime – she would scavenge the graveyard to collect body parts. To confirm her story, the authorities searched the cemetery for evidence of grave robbing. Her diary told of how she used the body parts in her potions and spells. Just imagine – a pinch of kidney and a slice of brain mixed with two fingers to create an endless sleep."

■ Centre 6 – Collecting 'Monster Teeth'

Object of the game:	To collect the most monster teeth (white beans) in your team's bowl
Number of players:	2 teams of equal number
Materials:	

- 2 bowls
- 2 chairs
- 1 table
- 2 lbs (1 kg) of dry white beans
- masking tape
- 2 pails
- 2 spoons
- candy treats for all players

Setup

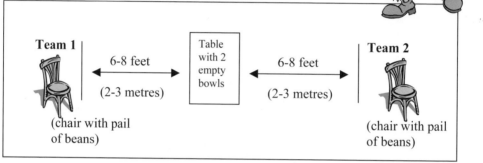

Team 1   ←— 6-8 feet —→   Table with 2 empty bowls   ←— 6-8 feet —→   **Team 2**

(2-3 metres)   (2-3 metres)

(chair with pail of beans)   (chair with pail of beans)

To Assemble:
1. Put two empty bowls on a table in the centre of the room (one for each team).
2. Make a line with tape on opposite sides of the table, an equal distance from the table (approximately 6-8 feet) for each team.
3. Place a small pail of white beans (monster teeth) on each team's chair, which is positioned behind their line.

To Play:
1. Have players line up single-file at their chair, facing the table.
2. Start the clock on the signal 'Ready – Set – BOO'!
3. The first team member scoops out some monster teeth with a spoon and runs to the centre table to put in his team's bowl, WITHOUT dropping any monster teeth. If a player drops any teeth along the way, their turn is over and they must pass the spoon to the next player on their team, who then takes a turn.
4. Stop the clock when everyone has had at least one turn.
5. Count the beans in each bowl to determine the winning team.

Variation: rather than disqualifying a team member because they've dropped some teeth, let them finish and then you can remove the number of teeth they dropped. For instance, if they dropped three teeth, you also remove three teeth from their team's bowl.

Raising Kids...for the fun of it!

■ Centre 7 – Draw a Witch

Step 1 – Draw a triangle **Step 2** – Add the brim **Step 3** – draw her profile

Step 4 – Add wart on nose, eye and teeth **Step 5** – Add her hair **Step 6** – Add body

★ *"I learned the steps to draw this witch when I was in grade four. As an adult, I have taught my kids and their friends how to draw her and it's so easy everyone feels like a pro."* ★

The witch can be:
- flying on her broom
- stirring a cauldron
- casting a spell

■ Centre 8 – Halloween Word Scramble

When you need something to slow down the pace, give your guests a pencil and the following list of words to unscramble:

1. ghoul
2. trick
3. creatures
4. haunted
5. goblin
6. treat
7. scary
8. witch
9. pumpkin
10. ghost
11. Halloween
12. potion

1. HULGO _____
2. CIRKT _____
3. RUTSCAERE_____
4. NDUHEAT _____
5. BNIGOL_____
6. RATET_____
7. YCSAR _____
8. CTHIW_____
9. IMNPPKU_____
10. THOSG_____
11. NWEHLALEO_____
12. OPNOTI_____

Raising Kids…for the fun of it!

Connect with 'Family Meetings'

Do you find that you're often discussing and negotiating the same issues over and over again with your kids? Does your family unit sometimes lack cohesion? Is it difficult to find the opportunity to plan and make important decisions together? It takes time and effort for everyone to work towards a common understanding and to get *on the same page*. A family meeting is an effective way to discuss important issues and make decisions as a group. The entire family becomes clear about the rules, routines and expectations.

Family Meetings Provide Opportunities

- problem solve and negotiate
- share individual feelings and concerns
- make family decisions
- coordinate schedules
- assign tasks
- plan fun activities and vacations
- pay allowance (optional)

> ★ *"I was a little apprehensive as we began our first family meeting. How would it go and would the kids respond to our questions and to the discussion? But the kids acted so grown up as they sat down to a meeting with a real agenda. Many of their solutions for the issues were very mature, they seemed to sense the importance of their contribution. The meeting went so well, we set the date for the next one, just two weeks later."* ★

Agenda

Use an informal agenda that basically lists topics of concern in point form. The agenda should be kept in a handy location, like on the fridge where everyone in the family will have access to it. This allows anyone to add important topics that they feel need discussion at the next meeting.

Topics – November 10
☑ Homework
☑ Allowance
☑ Christmas break – holiday plans

Kids Introduce Topics

Kids are welcome to include their areas of concern on the agenda. Give them an opportunity to state their case and offer viable solutions to consider.

★ *"When my son was 12 years old he realized that his allowance would not cover the purchase of sports equipment and computer games. So he wrote 'allowance' on the agenda. At the next family meeting he introduced the topic and explained why it was important to him. He convinced us that he needed a raise. We decided to increase his allowance and also his household tasks. He left the meeting feeling that his opinion was important and ready to take on his new responsibilities."* ★

Team Building

One of the main functions of a family meeting is to solve important issues. Your family will feel like a 'team', as they discuss a problem and work together to find a solution. Be sure everyone has a chance to give their opinion or offer their ideas, so each family member feels like a 'team player'.

★ *"Homework was becoming a constant battle in our household. The kids were procrastinating so long each night that homework often became the last thing done. It seemed there were too many activities or play dates that got in the way, too much time on the computer or watching TV or too many phone calls. My husband and I found ourselves constantly reminding, coercing or nagging the children to get at their homework. Something had to change! So we planned a family meeting and homework was the first agenda item. Our family discussed how homework was negatively affecting many evenings in our lives. Next, we talked about the result of doing homework so late that it was often not their best work since they were too tired or too rushed to do a good job. Everyone admitted what a problem it had become and how it created tension in our home. We discussed different options and finally came up with a unified decision. Once everyone was home from school they'd have a short break and a snack and then immediately get to their homework. After the homework was finished each child was free to do whatever they'd like. This particular group decision literally transformed our home life. We were not arguing anymore or constantly negotiating. We all felt a sense of relief; even the children expressed how nice it was not to have homework and studying hanging over their heads all evening and how great it feels to get it out of the way. Dealing with this issue in a family meeting was very effective for us."* ★

Raising Kids…for the fun of it!

Running the Meeting

Take notes or minutes during the meeting. Keep the minutes brief, they serve as a reminder of the discussions that took place and the decisions that were made. When a resolution to an issue is written down everyone takes it more seriously. Also, the entire family has a place to look for the information at a later date if needed. For instance, if someone has forgotten what the family decided about homework routines, instead of reiterating the decision to them verbally, you can pull out the family meeting notebook and let the children look for themselves.

> *Use a scribbler labelled 'Family Meetings' to record the minutes.*

Initially, one parent will guide the meeting and the other will take the minutes. This can be done until everyone gets comfortable with how the meetings are run and the children are ready to take a turn as the secretary.

Notes from meeting on November 10

1. Decisions made:
   - Homework is done as soon as you are home from school; no play dates or TV until it is finished.
   - Derek will receive an increase in allowance to $12.00 / week.
   - Christmas Break Plans – budget and plan for a trip to Auntie's

2. Responsibilities:

   For Peter:
   Daily
   unload dishwasher
   feed & water pet
   Weekly
   clean pet cage

   For Derek:
   Daily
   set & clear table
   take out garbage
   Weekly
   clean the washroom

3. Allowance paid ✓

Make Your Meeting a Success

Make your first family meeting a positive experience:
- Prior to the meeting discuss any major issues with your spouse to make sure you are both in agreement with each other.
- Inform the children that there will be a family meeting. Choose a time when everyone is at their best and have your pen, scribbler and calendar ready.
- Begin by explaining why you are having a family meeting and that you'd like their input into some important family matters. Be sure to

use meeting time for 'team building', with plenty of positive reinforcement.

- If you are discussing a touchy subject, be mindful of how you introduce it. Blaming or being negative will make family members defensive and the conversation will not begin well. Use observations of what is taking place in your home rather than naming a particular family member or members that may be creating the problem.
- Try to keep the meeting to about a half-hour. If an issue is quite in-depth and taking up a lot of time, it may need to be saved until the next meeting. Sometimes after a discussion you may find an issue does not pertain to the whole family. If so, try a one-on-one parent and child discussion once everyone has had a chance to regroup and think it over.
- A family meeting can be less formal and still be an effective setting for raising issues, solving problems and setting plans as a family. It is not compulsory to write out an agenda and keep minutes in order to have a successful family meeting. Try out different formats and decide which approach works best for your family.

> Host meetings with special foods your family enjoys like muffins and a fruit plate.

★ *"Our family dynamics had taken a turn for the worse. There were unkind words being spoken, disapproving and sarcastic looks being given to each other and the tone of voice being used was unacceptable. The situation was escalating and almost becoming a habit. I felt it had to stop. When I introduced the topic at a family meeting I was careful not to single anyone out. I said that I did not like the negative tone around our house and that it was not a good way for a family to operate. I asked everyone to list on a sheet of paper observations of what they had seen happening in our home that wasn't acceptable and that hurt them. Everyone in the family immediately understood and began listing what they saw taking place, such as tone of voice, teasing and sarcasm. Once these were written down we had a great place to start. The issue was out in the open and everyone could clearly see how serious it had become. Secondly, I asked everyone to write down how they wanted other family members to treat them. Finally, the third part involved each person describing what they would personally do to improve the situation. The way in which I introduced the topic had set a positive tone for our discussion and we were ready to find a solution."* ★

Raising Kids...for the fun of it!

Winter

Create the Christmas of Your Dreams

Take a minute and dream… Think about the perfect Christmas for you and your family. What would it look like? How would you feel? What would you be doing? Where would you be spending your time and with whom? Now ask yourself, *'How is this picture different from the reality of last Christmas season?'* If your 'Dream Christmas' has a calmer, less hectic pace, with more time for family activities and visiting, then read on.

While many people will promise to 'start earlier' or 'get organized,' you really need to ask yourself and your family a more basic question first. Are we spending our time on the things that are important to us during the Christmas season?

★ *"Christmas two years ago was the final straw. I ran around frantically buying gifts, making two trips to the same store because I'd forgotten to pick up something, and fell into bed each night exhausted. I attended my daughter's concert and when she asked which was my favourite song, I couldn't remember which ones they sang because I was thinking of all the things I still had to do to get ready for Christmas. I had such a bad cold over the Christmas break I couldn't enjoy the family activities. I vowed to change, to have a calmer, more relaxed Christmas, to find balance. This year I chose to attend fewer activities, but decided to really enjoy them, to be present in body and in mind. Sure there are lots of things on my 'to do' list that I must do like buying gifts, sending cards, baking cookies, and decorating the tree. But some things are within my control and I can choose to drop them off the list. I learned to say no to some invitations, to make things less elaborate and to enlist the help of my family with some of the preparations. The peaceful atmosphere and sense of calm it brought, created our best Christmas ever."* ★

The First Step

Have a family discussion where everyone gets to identify a couple of things they really want to do this Christmas season. Talk it over and discover which elements of the Christmas season are important to each of you. Maybe your family doesn't need 6 different kinds of home baked cookies, but would be satisfied with shortbread and nanaimo bars. You may be surprised to discover your kids really *don't* like to get their picture taken with Santa at the mall or that your husband really *does* want to hear a choir sing carols.

The Second Step

Adjust your attitude. The Christmas season has grown into this huge machine that takes an incredible amount of energy and time to keep running. If you are resolved to create more calm and less stress during the season you may need to drop some things from your list. Perhaps this is the year you stop sending Christmas cards to local friends that you'll see over the holidays or shorten your shopping list by picking names in your extended family or circle of friends.

The Third Step

Create a calm enjoyable Christmas season through planning and organization. Anything that you can do early will mean less to do at the last minute, freeing up your time to relax and delight in the season. Bake a batch of shortbread cookies, prepare several recipes of your favourite appetizer and then store them in the freezer. Start your Christmas cards weeks before they need to be mailed. Bit by bit you'll be chipping away at your 'to do' list. When the full impact of the season hits, you'll have many things already done and be able to enjoy the activities with family and friends a lot more.

> ***Extra cash*** *– Are your children looking for some extra spending money for Christmas shopping? It's your perfect opportunity to create a list of chores in exchange for cash. This may also help you get some Christmas tasks completed.*

Raising Kids…for the fun of it!

Get Organized for Christmas

Each year many mothers shudder at the thought of getting ready for the Christmas season. Gifts, food, cards, decorations and entertaining can put you into a frenzy. One key to a calm Christmas is being organized. Start early and use the methods below to help you get control of the holiday season.

Start a Christmas Binder

One method to getting organized for the holidays is to have a binder where all the Christmas lists, notes and recipes can be found. Call it the 'Christmas Binder' and use it from year to year. Use sheet protectors for those items you want grouped together and items that you don't want to hole punch.

★ *"I have tried many methods over the years to get organized for the Christmas season. My current approach has evolved over time and is by far my favourite because it is so simple. I have a 'Christmas Binder'. It contains my recipes, card list, shopping lists, and our family calendar of events for the season. My whole family loves having one place to look for all the Christmas information. An added bonus is being able to reference last year's information when planning for this year."* ★

Get a Handle on Your Schedule

Copy blank calendar sheets for November and December.
- Write in any concerts or parties you plan to attend.
- Identify the date that the out-of-town gifts must be mailed.
- Choose a deadline for your cards to be mailed by.
- Be sure to schedule activities that are important to your family, like hearing your favourite choir, donating time to a local charity or driving around to see Christmas lights.

★ *"One woman I know sets an artificial Christmas deadline of December 15th. She has all her preparations complete and then can thoroughly enjoy the days leading up to Christmas."* ★

- Choose dates where your children are available to help with as many tasks as possible. This will help lessen your work load, and will also allow them to learn what's involved in creating a calm and controlled Christmas season.

Create a Plan for Christmas Foods

- **Create a list of favourite foods.** Your family will have special foods they enjoy during the Christmas season. Ask each family member to list one item they would like for the Christmas meal and which one or two treats are special to them at Christmas time. Consider purchasing some pre-packaged items to increase your selection, rather than making your home-made list too long.
- **Prepare foods in advance.** Write specific dates on the calendar when you will prepare items that can be made in advance and frozen. Consider working with a friend to prepare foods ahead; you'll stock up your freezer fast.

Effective Gift Shopping

Try these techniques for getting the Christmas shopping done quickly.

1. **Create a complete gift list** with all the names of people you need to buy for: relatives, friends, teachers, paperboy, cleaning lady, dance instructor and hairdresser, and even include a couple of general hostess gifts. If you have birthdays to buy for in December include those names on your shopping list too.

2. **Jot down any gift ideas** you have in mind for a specific person. For gift ideas, go through flyers and catalogues, considering the recipient's hobbies and interests. If you're having a hard time generating some gift ideas at this point, ask your family for their input or even ask the recipient.

3. **Identify out of town gifts** that need to be purchased, wrapped and mailed. These need to take priority as mailing deadlines won't wait.

4. **Mark your calendar** with a target date by which **all** gifts must be purchased. Decide how many shopping trips you can realistically fit into the time you have.

5. **Group the gifts** by gender, age or proximity of the stores. For example, one night you shop for the men on your list (clothes, tools, cologne, publications), another night is kids' stuff (toys, games, clothes, memberships or lessons, gift certificates).

> *Choose the perfect gift for an adult.*
> - *Do some research. Really think about the person receiving the gift – what is their favourite hobby or pastime? Are there any sports, authors or movie stars that they are crazy about? Is there a special restaurant or food item they really enjoy?*
> - *Choose something consumable – aromatherapy candle, herbal tea, special candy or jam.*
> - *Try a stress relieving gift – wind chimes, Zen garden or a gift certificate to a spa or exercise club.*

Raising Kids…for the fun of it!

6. **Assign the shopping trips to specific dates**, with the items for mailing first and Christmas morning items later in the schedule.

7. **Don't get distracted when you go to the mall** and stick to your list. Remember your mission is to buy the gifts assigned to that shopping trip.

8. **Purchase gifts without leaving your home** by using catalogue shopping, mail order, internet shopping, phone ordering and subscriptions.

9. **Find one great idea** and use it for several people. Give many people on your list the same gift like a game, a book or flavored coffee and mugs. You could make a huge batch of caramel corn or an assembly line craft to give to each teacher, child's friend, hairdresser or hostess. With this strategy you only have to come up with one idea and you get several names checked off your list.

> **Keep Christmas Receipts Handy**
> *Put a red envelope in your purse and every time you purchase a gift, file the receipt into this handy storage place. Keep all your receipts for a full month after Christmas, to facilitate easy returns.*

> ★ *"One year my sister couldn't come home for Christmas, so we decided to send Christmas to her. We baked some of her favourite treats that would travel well in the mail, including biscotti and caramel corn. We borrowed a video camera and created a tape of the family singing 'We Wish you a Merry Christmas'. Then we included a few photos of the Christmas concert and of our house decorated for the season. A handmade Christmas tree ornament and greeting card completed the parcel. We enjoyed putting together her 'Christmas in a Box' and she was thrilled to receive it."* ★

Sample Calendar to Help With Your Christmas Planning

November

Sunday	Monday	Tuesday	Wednesday	Thursday	Friday	Saturday
	1	**2**	**3**	**4**	**5**	**6**
7	**8**	**9**	**10**	**11**	**12**	**13**
14 make Xmas cakes	**15** write Xmas letter	**16**	**17** gingerbread	**18**	**19**	**20** bake shortbread
21 shop men's gifts	**22** shop bookstore	**23** house decorations	**24**	**25** start craft	**26** craft	**27**
28 make spinach loaves	**29** make squares	**30**				

December

Sunday	Monday	Tuesday	Wednesday	Thursday	Friday	Saturday
			1	**2** shop teachers	**3** shop kids	**4** wrap gifts
5 decorate tree	**6** mail parcels	**7** address cards	**8** mail cards	**9** school concert	**10** staff party	**11** rest & recovery
12 wrap gifts	**13** see lights	**14** watch choir	**15** final shop	**16** take in teacher gift	**17** party prep	**18** host party
19 church concert	**20** visit with friends	**21**	**22** final wrap	**23** meal prep	**24**	**25** Christmas Day
26 p.j. day	**27**	**28** host a games nite	**29**	**30**	**31**	

Raising Kids...for the fun of it!

Can't locate all your little stocking stuffers? As you purchase stocking stuffers, remove tags and place them into bags, which you have labelled for each child. Keep the bags handy to add the little items purchased throughout the season.

Where can you safely hide those precious gifts until Christmas?
- *a plastic storage container in the trunk of your car*
- *large cardboard storage box in the garage*
- *a trunk in a crawl space or attic of your home*
- *under blankets or linens in a cedar chest*
- *behind towels in linen closet*
- *a closet in guest room or under the bed*
- *empty boxes from your Christmas decorations or your artificial tree*
- *empty suitcases*

Family Fun

Prepare for Christmas with a Friend

An important part of the Christmas season is spending time with friends. Here's a way to have fun together and fill your freezer too. Discuss this idea with a couple of friends and then decide whose kitchen to use and what you'll make. Baked goods and many appetizers freeze well, and come in very handy over the festive season.

■ Here are some tips to consider.

- Begin early in the season.
- Decide which recipes you'd like to make together.
- Go through each recipe and determine what ingredients you'll need.
- Buy in bulk to save money.
- Split the shopping list and share the costs involved.
- Divide the list of the tools and supplies you'll need to bring on baking day: baking pans, sharp knives, cutting boards, mixer, food processor, plastic wrap, aluminum foil, wax paper, tin containers or zipper bags for storing finished food items you've prepared.

★ *"When my girlfriend told me she had four spinach loaves in her freezer ready for the festive season, I was amazed. I had never considered making appetizers ahead of time and freezing them. She had invited over a couple of friends one Saturday afternoon and made them together. They had such fun they were planning a Christmas baking bee too."* ★

Home-made doesn't necessarily mean made in YOUR home—try these sources for great home-made food to add to your selection.

- Community craft and bake sales
- Farmer's market
- Church bazaar
- Local community college where cooking training is offered
- Independent caterers

Serving and Presentation
Add some pre-packaged foods to supplement your platter. Not everything needs to be home-made to be enjoyed. There are many good quality products now available that will lighten your baking load. For example, add chocolate peppermint patties, fine quality chocolates and fancy imported cookies to your dessert tray.

Store each kind of home baked item separately.
Tins work better than plastic containers for maintaining the original flavour and texture of baked goods.

An alternative to a baking bee is a 'baking swap'.
Organize a Christmas squares or cookie swap. For example, invite three friends and create a list of a variety of squares (like lemon, three layer or date) that all the families enjoy. Then each person chooses two recipes from those listed and makes three batches of each kind. Pick a date to get together to distribute equal amounts of each item. Enjoy a visit and go home with a selection of six different home baked treats to stock your freezer.

Organized Living

Christmas Shopping Together

Is it possible for you and your spouse to each take a day off from work and spend it together? Plan your shopping day in advance; decide what presents you'll buy, what route to take and the order of the stops. The stores will be less crowded during the day, compared to evening or weekend shopping trips. Enjoy each other's company while tackling the Christmas gift list together.

★ *"Initially when I asked my husband to take a day off work to Christmas shop it was because I really needed the help. I soon discovered the many advantages of his involvement. The two of us got the job done quicker, he felt more involved and we felt more connected by working together. It ended up being a really great day and a positive start to our busy festive season."* ★

Dealing with Your Child's Gift Desires

At Christmas it can be difficult for children to avoid a case of 'the gimmees'. Advertisers are expert at creating interest, leading to a strong yearning for too many things. As the flyers bombard the mailbox and the Christmas commercials increase, children's gift desires build. Here are some positive ways to deal with the situation.

■ For younger children, a wish book is ideal.

Let them design their own cover and staple several unlined sheets inside. As the flyers come in, have them cut out their favourite items and glue them into the wish book. Every time they say '*I want…*,' you reply with '*Put it in your wish book*'.

■ For older children, a collage or wish list is great.

Have kids cut out items from flyers and glue them on to a piece of coloured paper, overlapping the edges. Or they can create a wish list that includes the store and the price of the items. The compilation of gift ideas will not just be useful for parents but often grandmas and aunties or uncles are asking for gift ideas too. You can simply go to their wish book or collage for reference.

> ★ *"When my daughter was very young she started a Christmas wish list. Whenever she saw something on TV or at the store that she wanted I didn't argue with her, I simply said, 'What a great idea, put it on your wishlist'. She knew she wouldn't necessarily get it, but it gave her a positive outlet for those desires."* ★

■ Turn their attention to the 'giving aspect of Christmas'.

You can also encourage your children to include a page or two in their wish book or a section on their wish list for others. As they are looking through flyers or catalogues it may prompt ideas for people on their gift list. It is the perfect time to cut out the idea or to write it down to purchase later.

> ★ *"One Mom I know takes her children to the toy store in November, each carrying their own clipboard and pencil. They go up and down the aisles stopping to check out items of interest. She encourages the children to check out the item and ask themselves how well made it is and will it do what the ad says. After careful assessment, if they still want the toy they write it on their clipboard gift list."* ★

Organized Living

Kid's Gift Ideas

It seems the majority of our gift giving throughout the year is for children and we are always on the hunt for that 'perfect' gift. Use this comprehensive list as a reference any time you need to spark your imagination for a great gift for some lucky child.

■ Tickets:

- live theatre performance
- horse show, dog show
- movie pass
- movie rental or gift certificate
- sports game, such as university, college, high school or professional teams

■ Books:

- bug book
- nature or bird identification book
- cassette and read-along book
- puzzles and brain-teasers
- comic or joke book
- book of card games; include a crib board and a deck of cards
- book of string games, like 'Cats in the Cradle'
- diary and fancy pen

■ Magazine subscription for:

- Owl
- Stamp Quest
- Highlights
- Jr. Sports Illustrated

■ Make a theme basket:

- craft theme – include smelly markers, gel pens, a variety of cool paper, a pair of decorative scissors, glitter glue
- gardening theme – gloves, seeds, plant pot and a book on gardening
- bath theme – animal soaps, special face cloth, washable graffiti crayon, funnels, sponges
- watercolour painter's basket – watercolour paper, paints, brushes, sketch pad

> ★ *"My gift cupboard has saved me a shopping trip more than once. When I find a great gift at a good price I often buy two and tuck one away in the 'gift cupboard'. It's especially handy when we've received short notice to a party."* ★

■ Gift certificate for lessons:

- horseback riding
- watercolour painting

Raising Kids...for the fun of it!

■ Kits and crafty items:

- jewelry making
- birdhouse
- fridge magnets
- science experiments
- pillowcase or t-shirt and some fabric paints
- make a batch of play dough, include the recipe, cookie cutters, garlic press or mini rolling pin for a variety of tools to use with the play dough

■ Sporty items:

- juggling balls with instructions
- package of tennis balls
- skipping rope, yo-yo and a bag of marbles for recess
- sport pendant

■ Board games:

- Trouble or Sorry
- Charades or Guesstures
- a smaller travel version of a board game

■ For collectors:

- sports cards (hockey, baseball, basketball)
- binder with plastic pockets
- books by authors they enjoy
- coins or stamps
- figurines or animals

★ *"My son loves dolphins. Last year I gave him a dolphin figurine for his room and he was thrilled. Since that time, he has expanded his collection to posters, calendars and a dolphin picture frame. Now when relatives or friends ask for a gift idea, I'll often suggest adding to his dolphin collection."* ★

■ Other ideas:

- disposable camera, film and small photo album
- funky umbrella
- beach towel
- real wallet or purse
- dollar store jewelry, hats or wigs for a dress-up box
- wall poster
- music CD or tape
- newly released video, complete with a bag of microwave popcorn and a can of their favourite soft drink

Family Fun

Count Down to Christmas

Try this personalized Advent calendar idea as a clever way to present tasks and activities throughout the Christmas season. Buy or make a calendar and tuck in daily notes to entice the kids. Occasionally add a treat or small gift. The notes can be as simple as a sentence to give a preview of the day or a short poem to add a little flair. Throw in a festive joke or two along the way for a little variety. Use the following examples for your family this December or modify them to suit your day-to-day activities.

Fun Little Poems ━━━━━━━━━━━━━━━

Using poems as you count down to Christmas can add a little fun to everyday tasks or activities.

December 2
December the second, isn't it grand?
I wonder what Mom and Dad have planned?
The Christmas letter, it's time to write.
And drink hot chocolate to complete
the night.

December 3
Today, dear friends, is December the third.
What's on today? Give me the word.
Buy Grandma's gift,
it'll be special for sure.
Then we'll wrap it and get it
mailed off to her.

December 18
This is the season for fun & good cheer.
What are we doing as Christmas gets near?
It's something special & really
quite neat.
We're going to watch the Nutcracker Suite.

December 19
December 19th, time is going so fast.
Pretty soon the month will have gone past.
A favourite tradition with friends is today.
Decorate gingerbread houses
and play!

December 20
Good morning kids, are you feeling keen?
Get your muscles ready to clean! clean!
clean!
Company is coming, things must be just so.
It won't be long 'til we hear Santa's,
        'Ho! Ho! Ho!'

December 24
The 24th is a very exciting day.
Long ago Mary & Joseph were
on their way.
A miracle happened, for many a reason.
Baby Jesus was born,
the best gift of the season!

Raising Kids…for the fun of it!

★ *"Our family began using an Advent calendar several years ago. All through December, it is the first thing the boys go to in the morning. They love to read the notes and poems about what is happening each day. When the kids were young, it seemed like such a long time 'til Christmas morning—the Advent calendar with its little notes and wishes helped them deal with the waiting period. It continues to be a favourite tradition in our home."* ★

Short Notes

Using just a simple sentence of what's happening for the day can help everyone get ready for an activity, a task that must be done or prepare themselves for an errand that has to be run.

December 1
Today we put out our Nativity scene.

December 2
Get out your Christmas gift list, we're going shopping for presents today.

December 3
It's Saturday night; we'll decorate the Christmas tree and enjoy some eggnog with cookies.

December 4
Today's the day we help wrap gifts for Santa's Anonymous.

December 5
Tonight is the Christmas concert at school. We can't wait to see you perform!

December 6
Tonight we'll go for a for a drive and look at the Christmas lights.

You don't have to fill all the pockets before December 1, just be sure you've stuffed in your note and a little candy before they check!

Christmas Jokes

Add a little variety and humour by putting a joke in some pockets of your Advent calendar.

Why does Santa go down the chimney?

...*Because it soots him.*

What's Santa's favourite cereal?

... *Frosted Flakes.*

Where does Frosty the snowman keep his money?

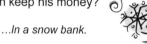

...*In a snow bank.*

What do you call Santa when he has no money?

...*Saint Nickel-less.*

What do you get when you cross a snowman with a shark?

...*Frostbite*

What did Mrs. Claus say to Santa during the storm?

...*Come and look at the rain, dear.*

Customized Advent Notes

Create a wonderful gift for Grandparents or friends with an Advent calendar they'll treasure.

★ *"One year at Christmas, we made an Advent calendar for our grandparents. In each calendar pocket we placed a candy or mint, along with a special message we had written. We planned on creating new messages and adding new treats each year. But when we checked with Grandma the next fall, she said there was no need to restock the pockets. She had enjoyed the little notes so much that she had saved them all."* ★

Raising Kids...for the fun of it!

It's the 1st of December,
and Christmas is near.
Better start your list,
before Christmas is here.

Grandma, don't forget to bake
the shortbread cookies for Dad.
Because they're the best
that he's ever had!

We've practised our singing,
our verses are cool.
Grandpa & Grandma you're invited
to our Christmas concert
at school.

Here's 2 candy canes
for you to share.
Or hang them up
on your tree with care.

Mistletoe, holly,
decorations galore.
Did you remember to hang,
your wreath by the door?

Turkey and gravy,
potatoes and peas.
For Grandma's great meal,
we'll all say 'please'.

Family Fun

Create a Curtain of Gingerbread

This traditional treat has a unique twist when you hang these wrapped cookies in your window. You create a curtain of gingerbread when individually wrapped cookies are connected in long vertical rows. Follow these step-by-step instructions to decorate and display these treats, which are perfect for sharing with your guests at Christmas.

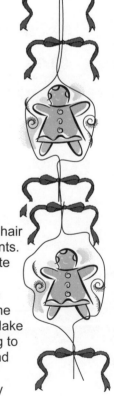

1. **To begin, mix up your favourite gingerbread dough recipe and use cookie cutters to shape the dough into gingerbread men and women.**
- Once the cookies are ready for the oven, you can get creative by tilting the head, waving the arms or bending the legs.
- Bake as directed by your recipe. Or, if you are short on time buy pre-made cookies.

What you'll need:
- gingerbread men and women
- royal icing or stiff butter icing
- plastic zipper sandwich bags
- food colouring
- large needle
- m & m's mini baking variety
- baking sprinkles

- silver ball baking decorations
- 2 or 3 colours of melting chocolate
- strong packaging tape
- curling ribbon ¼" (5mm) wide cut into 10" (25cm) strips
- strong plastic wrap
- garland (for the width of your window)

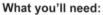

2. **Decorate your gingerpeople.**
- Use melted chocolate – It's easy to dress up your cookies with just a few colours of melted chocolate. Spread on brown chocolate for the hair and boots, try red for the hats and mitts, and green for dresses or pants. You can dip a hand in chocolate to create a mitt, or dip a foot to create a boot. The chocolate leaves a smooth glossy texture.
- Use icing – Outlines and details are created with the icing. Prepare and divide one batch of icing into three plastic zipper bags. Leave one bag white, color another yellow and the third one purple (or blue). Make a tiny hole in the corner of the bag to push the icing through as piping to decorate. Or the icing can also be used as 'glue' to hold sprinkles and other decorations.
- Add sprinkles and other decorations – create eyes, buttons or jewelry with candy adornments.

Raising Kids…for the fun of it!

Examples of gingerbread characters. Once the eyes, nose and mouth are piped onto the basic gingerbread, use your imagination to create a variety of characters:

- **Dancer** – made from a gingerbread woman. Create a dress with coloured chocolate. Pipe on a white necklace and try a single silver ball as a pearl necklace.
- **Santa** – use a knife to spread on a red chocolate suit and then create the hat by dipping the top of the head in red chocolate. Use the white icing to pipe a pompom and band on the hat, and then add a long curly white beard and moustache. Place a few shiny silver balls down Santa's suit as buttons. Dip hands and feet in brown chocolate to create boots and mitts. You can even add a belt and buckle.
- **Mrs. Claus** – squeeze some icing from the bag around the edge of her head to make curly hair. Spread on some chocolate to create a dress, use icing to outline her apron and to add a ruffle to the bottom of her dress.

3. **Create your gingerbread curtain for your window.**
   - Allow the icing to dry thoroughly.
   - Place long vertical rows of plastic wrap on the kitchen table. Each strip should measure 12" (30 cm) longer than the length of your window.
   - Place the first gingerbread facedown in the middle of the plastic wrap approximately 8" (20 cm) from the top of the plastic.
   - Continue to place gingerbread cookies facedown in a vertical row on the plastic wrap, leaving 6" (15 cm) between each cookie.
   - Fold over the long sides of the plastic wrap to cover the gingerbread cookies.
   - Tie a curling ribbon at the top and bottom of every cookie, making each cookie individually wrapped and tied so it can be easily cut off the row.
     Each row is completed as follows:
     - 8" (20 cm) of plastic wrap at the top for taping to the window
     - curling ribbon tied in a knot
     - gingerbread
     - curling ribbon tied in a knot
     - 6" (15 cm) of space
     - repeat to desired length

4. **Hang the vertical rows of gingerbread.**
   - Attach the rows of gingerbread onto the top of the window using strong packaging tape or duct tape.
   - Cover the tape with a festive spray of fir tree garland.

5. **Your gingerbread are ready for sharing.**
   - Tie a decorative ribbon on a pair of scissors and keep them near the window. The gingerbread is ready to be given as little parting gifts to guests who visit your home throughout the festive season.

Variation: Once you have mastered the creation of these wonderful cookie treats you may want to try more elaborate figures. If you are baking your own cookies you can add a soccer ball, golf club, dumbbells or other embellishments to 'bake in' added personality. When adding extra parts make the dough slightly thicker to allow for it to be pressed onto the initial figure, so that it bakes as one piece. Before baking you'll be able to create:

- **Weightlifter** – add dough muscles to the arms and legs, bend the knees into a 'weightlifter's squat'. Make a dumbbell or two and place in the hands. Decorate with icing or chocolate to add a pair of shorts, and suspenders.
- **Soccer player** – add a soccer ball to the foot of your gingerbread. Paint on a jersey with the chocolate and use icing to pipe on her player number.
- **Hockey player** – roll a 'snake' of dough, press it flat and bend the end at an angle to create a hockey stick.

★ *"Each year, we look forward to spending family time together baking and decorating gingerbread cookies. We have been enjoying this Christmas tradition for about five years, and it has grown into a favourite with our boys, David and Matthew. The gingerbread taste wonderful, and look great when we display them in the window by our door. We especially love the reaction we get when friends come to visit during the holidays. As guests approach our house, they see the 'curtain' of gingerbread decorating the window. Upon entering our home, the fragrance of ginger and cinnamon greets them. Once our visit is complete and it's time for our guests to leave, we ask them to choose any cookie from the bottom of the rows to take with them. We have found that no matter how old our guests are they're thrilled to receive the beautifully decorated, yummy, home-baked treat."* ★

Raising Kids...for the fun of it!

Family Fun

Play 'Christmas Carol Trivia'

When travelling to the shopping mall or while waiting for Christmas concerts or other events, play a game of Christmas Carol Trivia.

■ Christmas Carol Questions

1. What are they decorating the halls with?
2. What did the night wind say to the shepherd boy?
3. What is roasting on an open fire?
4. What did the king say to the people everywhere?
5. What did your true love give you on the sixth day?
6. What did your true love give you on the eleventh day?
7. In 'Joy to the World' who is singing with heaven?
8. Name the eight reindeer not including Rudolph.
9. What kind of pudding is requested in 'We Wish you a Merry Christmas'?
10. Who was Mommy kissing under the mistletoe?
11. What are you dreaming of?
12. Where is Santa Claus coming?
13. What three gifts did the wise men bring?
14. Who is the young percussion lad?
15. What happened to Frosty at the end of the day?

Trivia answers:
1. holly
2. 'Do you see what I see?'
3. chestnuts
4. 'Listen to what I say'
5. six geese a-laying
6. eleven pipers piping
7. nature
8. Dasher, Dancer, Prancer, Vixen, Comet, Cupid, Donder, Blitzen
9. figgy
10. Santa Claus
11. a white Christmas
12. to town
13. gold, frankincense and myrrh
14. the little drummer boy
15. he melted away

> **Bedtime Delight**
> *Add sparkle and delight to your child's room at Christmas by placing a string of mini lights around their headboard, or place the lights in the shape of a Christmas tree on the wall by their bed.*

Snowman Gift Tags

Create adorable snowman gift tags that double as personalized tree ornaments. They make a lovely decoration on any wrapped gift and are a keepsake too. Get the whole family involved to make several holiday gift tags with this simple and fun craft idea.

1. **Paint both sides of the tongue depressors white.** Then allow them to dry.

2. **Make a loop for the ornament to hang on the tree.**
   - Cut a 14" (36 cm) piece of thin twine, fold in half and tie a knot at the bottom.
   - Glue the knot onto the back of the tongue depressor, 1" (2.5 cm) from the top.

3. **Make the hat from the felt or wool fabric.**
   - Cut a 2½" x 3½" (6 x 9 cm) rectangle.
   - Place the bottom of the fabric 1" (2.5 cm) from the top, which allows about half of the fabric to be above the tongue depressor. Glue one side onto the center back of the tongue depressor.
   - Tightly wrap the fabric around the tongue depressor and glue the other side to hold it firmly in place.
   - To cinch the hat together, cut a 3" (8 cm) piece of twine and tie it just above the top of the tongue depressor.

> **What you'll need:**
> - tongue depressors
> - white craft paint for wood
> - felt or wool fabric
> - thin twine
> - cool melt glue gun
> - fabric printed with a miniature Christmas design
> - black and orange fine-tipped felt pens
> - glue sticks
> - scissors

4. **Draw on the face with felt markers.**
   - Draw the eyes, smile and three buttons using the black felt marker.
   - Use the orange felt pen to draw and colour in the carrot-shaped nose.

5. **Make the snowman's scarf.**
   - Using the miniature printed fabric, cut a strip of fabric 5" x 1/2" (13 x 1cm).
   - Tie the scarf in-between the snowman's face and buttons, secure with a double knot.
   - Trim the fabric ends at an angle.

Raising Kids…for the fun of it!

6. Write on the back of the gift tag with the felt marker or gel pen. Include the year on the back too.

Merry Christmas
Auntie

Love, Kim

★ *"Each year our family creates another ornament in our 'gift tag series'. It is the one Christmas craft we make together and has now become a family tradition. Not only is it a tradition to make them, but also for family and friends to receive them. My husband paints the wood, and drills any holes or cuts and bends the wire. The girls cut the fabric and paint on the faces. We have made a Santa, a Snowman, Reindeer and an Elf. The girls give them to their friends as Christmas gifts and we use them as gift tags for presents for grandparents, cousins, aunts and uncles. Christmas just wouldn't be complete without making our special gift tags."* ★

The 'Spirit of Giving'

Christmas is the perfect time of year to get into the 'spirit of giving'. Discuss with your children the importance of giving, and the feeling you get when you give of yourself. It is often difficult for children to understand that there are those less fortunate than they are. Try to explain that some people don't have the love and support of a family, good health, food or even a home. Reinforce the importance of helping those who are not as fortunate either by giving gifts of time or money. Decide with your children how they too can help those in need.

> ★ *"I felt frustrated trying to fit charity into our already over-scheduled December. Then, one day, I was chatting with a woman who said, 'Oh, I get all my big stuff done for Christmas by December 1st and then I've got the whole month to give where it's really needed'. This gave me a whole new perspective on how to fit charity into my schedule and it was great food for thought."* ★

Help as a Family

Decide as a family what to do and how you can help others who are less fortunate:

- Give toys and clothing to a shelter.
- Have your children donate some of their allowance money to the food bank, Unicef, Goodwill or another charity.
- Pack up the Christmas decorations you no longer use, purchase a few new ones and give the collection to a youth shelter.
- Put together a Christmas care-package for a family.
- Get involved with Santa's Anonymous to wrap or deliver gifts.
- Sponsor a family overseas; have your children send a Christmas card and letter to them.
- Put up decorations in a hospital or shelter.

> ★ *"Each Christmas for the past ten years, my husband shops for a turkey that he donates to an inner city dinner. Glenn likes to purchases the biggest turkey he can find. Then he brings it home, where I stuff it with my home-made dressing and roast it in the oven. On December 24th, he takes the morning off work to deliver the turkey and carve it for the people at the shelter. In the afternoon, my husband comes home feeling grateful and proud to be able to help someone in need."* ★

Help as a Group

Get together some friends, or members of a club, so you will be able to make a greater contribution and have more possibilities.

- Prepare and serve a meal in a soup kitchen.
- Take in enough toques and mittens or teddy bears for a whole class at an inner city school.
- Take blankets into a hostel.
- Do a 'Shoe Box Drive' for a youth shelter – fill shoeboxes with toiletries, games, books or items that youths would appreciate. Wrap and tag each box for the gender and age group.
- Go to a senior's complex or hospital and give gifts of time or talent – if you sing, dance, play an instrument or have another talent, arrange to put on a small performance for a group of people.

★ *"My daughter Laura and her friends have been taking dance classes and piano lessons for years. Last Christmas, Laura organized a talent show for seniors in a nearby nursing home. I knew the seniors would be thrilled watching the dances and listening to the songs, but I had no idea how much these girls would get out of the experience. After the performance the girls visited with the residents for a short while. The girls really understood what a difference they'd made to these folks."* ★

Remember the Elderly

Your elderly neighbours and seniors in lodges or nursing homes love to be remembered during the Christmas season. Many of them have few family members and would enjoy a gift of your time or service.

- Share a cup of tea.
- Play a game of cards.
- Deliver a poinsettia.
- Make them a Christmas ornament.
- Bake some cookies and deliver them.
- Run an errand.
- Shovel sidewalks.
- Address or write their Christmas cards for them.
- Decorate a window or tree with outdoor lights.

★ *"We have lived next door to our neighbours for many years. They are quite elderly and have no family living nearby. They are always interested in our children's activities and hobbies. We wanted to do something special for them this year. So, we invited them over for tea and Christmas cookies. The kids played the piano and showed them some school projects. We had a lovely visit."* ★

Family Fun

Share the Season With Friends

An important part of the Christmas season is spending time with friends. However, often there are so many tasks, activities and traditions that it leaves little time for visiting with friends. So, why not combine them? If you traditionally make a Christmas craft or decorate gingerbread houses with the kids, include some friends in this activity. Or host an appetizer dinner or an evening of Christmas carolling. Here are four activities that are designed for fun with friends.

> ★ *"One of our favourite traditions each Christmas is decorating gingerbread scenes. We especially enjoy this activity as we share it with another family. The kids talk about the event for days in anticipation. We usually have a potluck meal together and then get right into decorating. It has been fun to watch the construction and designs change and evolve. As the children have grown so have the gingerbread scenes."* ★

Create Gingerbread Scenes

This Christmas, don't just make a gingerbread house—make a house, a yard, make a whole scene! The house is small and simple, which allows attention to be also focused on the yard, expanding the possibilities for decorating. Your winter scene can include old-fashioned light posts, fir trees, fences and even an outdoor skating rink or igloo!

What you'll need per person:
- cardboard 12" (30 cm) square, per building
- tinfoil
- royal icing
- strong plastic sandwich bags
- small empty milk cartons, 1 cup (250 ml) size
- graham wafers
- decorations (see list)

Raising Kids...for the fun of it!

■ How to create your gingerbread scene:

1. **Make a base.** Cover stiff cardboard with tin foil.

2. **Prepare or buy white royal icing and place in plastic bags**. Make a tiny hole in a corner of the bag to push the icing through as piping. The icing is ready to be used as the 'glue' to hold everything in place or it can simply be spread on the house or the tinfoil as snow.

> **Decoration suggestions:**
> * raisins – door handles, rocks or bricks
> * Shreddies – roof shingles
> * Cheerios – trim on the roof
> * pretzels – fences, log cabins
> * M&M's or Smarties – roof, pathway
> * small candy canes – light posts
> * Christmas candies
> * white mini marshmallows – snowmen built with toothpicks or stacked to make an igloo
> * spearmint leaf candies – placed around the yard as trees
> * blue sprinkles – skating rink
>   *Shop in the bulk food section of a grocery store to purchase small amounts of interesting items to embellish your gingerbread creations.*

3. **Construct the gingerbread house**. Use a small milk carton as the framework for the construction of your building. Empty the milk carton, rinse it and then tape the opening closed. Spread icing on one side of the graham wafers and stick them on to the sides of the carton for the walls. You may also want to use the wafers as shingles on the roof or just spread icing across the roof and decorate it with candies.

> ★ *"This year my son chose red and green gummie worms from the bulk candy section. They were great for outlining the door on the house and the curved walkway."* ★

4. **Glue the house to the base.** Dab icing on the bottom of the structure and secure it in place on the cardboard base. Allow the building to set for a few minutes.

5. **Decorate.** Now you're ready to use your imagination to decorate the house and yard with icing and candies.

> *Create a **Christmas village**. Broaden your gingerbread designs to include a village of houses, a church, train station, stores or a school. Display the gingerbread buildings together and you'll have an entire village.*

> ★ *"It feels so good to get together with friends over the holidays. Instead of trying to cram everything in before Christmas, we postpone gingerbread decorating until the week between Christmas and New Year's."* ★

Make Mini Christmas Trees

Here's an attractive craft that can easily be done with a group of friends. These nifty trees are fun and easy to make, and you'll find the supplies at most department or craft stores. The kids will marvel at the creations they have made. They can keep their trees to decorate their house or use them as gifts for teachers, grandparents, neighbours or friends.

What you'll need to make 4 trees:
- 4 mini terra-cotta clay pots
- gold or silver paint – either spray paint or acrylic craft paint
- a sponge
- oasis (green floral sponge)
- knife
- low heat glue gun and glue sticks
- 1 strand of green fir garland (the type of wired garland used to decorate banisters, mantels or doorways)
- wire cutters
- 1 package Spanish moss

Tree decoration suggestions:
- miniature beads or buttons
- small wooden stars or other wooden decorations
- mini garland (the wire kind used for wrapping gifts)
- tiny decorations smaller than 1½" (3.5 cm) high
- for a country look; tear strips of miniature printed fabric in ¼" - ½" (1 - 1.5 cm) widths and tie them on to the trees as whimsical country bows

■ How to create your mini Christmas trees:

1. **Spray or sponge paint clay pot.** Allow it to dry.

2. **Cut oasis to fit into the clay pot.** Turn the pot upside down on top of the oasis and apply pressure to make an imprint of the pot on the oasis. Use the impression as a guide and cut the oasis with a knife to fit into your pot.

3. **Glue the oasis into the clay pot.**

4. **Make the tree.** Cut a 6" – 8" (15 – 20 cm) piece off the garland. Shape the wire garland into 'branches' to create a tree and trim as needed.

5. **Secure the tree in place.** Apply glue to the bottom of the tree and push it into the middle of the oasis in the clay pot.

6. **Hide the oasis.** Spread glue over the oasis and cover it with Spanish moss.

7. **Decorate the tree.** Glue on your choice of mini decorations.

Raising Kids...for the fun of it!

Host an 'Appetizer' Dinner Party

During the festive season spend an evening with family or friends without the fuss of preparing a full meal. Have everyone bring a couple of appetizers to contribute to the dinner buffet. This casual, laid-back affair allows you to focus on the visit, not the endless preparations— enjoy your evening!

Possibilities for an appetizer dinner party:

veggies & dip
antipasto & crackers
mini quiches
chicken wings
shrimp ring

sausage rolls
spinach dip
cheese tray
honey garlic ribs
bruschetta

fruit tray
chocolates
Christmas baking

sparkling water
non-alcohol wine
wine
egg nog
cranberry punch
mulled apple cider

> ★ *"We love to get together with friends over the Christmas season, but we often had a hard time fitting it in amongst our other commitments. The thought of making a meal and entertaining was just too much. So a friend suggested an appetizer meal. It was perfect! We had plenty of food without all the planning and preparation."* ★

Go Christmas Carolling

Spend an evening Christmas carolling with your family, friends and neighbours. This old-fashioned Christmas activity is sure to foster good relations and kindle the Christmas spirit. Try these suggestions to help ensure your evening is a success.

> ★ *"One snowy evening in December, a group of neighbours joined our family to go carolling and spread some Christmas cheer throughout the neighbourhood. The night began with appetizers and mulled wine at our house where we met and practiced a few songs. Imagine the surprise and delight of our neighbours when they heard singing carollers at their door. At one house a lady was so moved she broke into tears, then happily got her coat on and joined in the carolling. At another house a family brought their sleepy, pajama-clad kids to the door and they responded to the singing with a rousting rendition of 'We wish you a Merry Christmas!' The evening ended with toasted marshmallows and hot chocolate, around a bonfire. We all had a great time sharing the Christmas spirit and bonding with our neighbours."* ★

1. **Invite neighbours to come for an evening of carolling.** Suggest they bring beverages or an appetizer to share.

2. **Get song sheets from your local newspaper.** Have one copy per person.

3. **Gather for a half hour of practice.**
   - Serve the appetizers and some beverages before you go carolling.
   - Begin singing practice with an easy children's song to encourage everyone's participation.
   - Consider singing only the easiest and most familiar parts of a song, usually the first verse and the chorus.
   - Choose a song or two that your group sings well and sing it from house to house.

4. **Take along a flashlight, candles or a lantern.**

Easy Songs for Caroling
- Jingle Bells
- We Wish you a Merry Christmas
- Hark the Herald Angels Sing
- Silent Night
- Deck the Halls
- Rudolph the Red-Nosed Reindeer
- Santa Claus is Coming to Town

Raising Kids…for the fun of it!

5. **Add musical instruments.** For fun include some jingle bells, triangles or tambourines to accompany the singing.

6. **Bring the camera and take lots of pictures.**

7. **Wrap up the evening with a visit.** When you return to your house enjoy some food, drink and fellowship with your neighbours.

★ *"Our girls wake us up each Christmas morning and sing 'We Wish You a Merry Christmas' before we all head downstairs to see what Santa has brought us. I love watching their faces as they open their stockings and read the note Santa left behind. I encourage them to savor each beautiful package before they reveal its contents. I really tried this year to soak in all the excitement and joy we were sharing as a family. All of the planning, shopping, decorating, baking and cooking was culminating today— Christmas Day. And I was choosing to really just enjoy it. There were a couple things that didn't get done, oh well, Christmas arrived and was wonderful anyway."* ★

Merry Christmas

Make Boxing Day A P.J. Day

The rush of the season is over; the gifts are bought, wrapped and mailed away, the turkey is cooked and half eaten, the house is cleaned and decorated. So, just relax! Don't even get dressed this Boxing Day—laze around in your pajamas. Relax and enjoy your new games, puzzles, toys and books all day long.

★ *"One Boxing Day we were having so much fun with the kids and their new toys that it was almost 5:00 before we realized we were still in our pajamas. That's how our tradition of Pajamas on Boxing Day got started."* ★

A Special Christmas Album

Gather all your pictures from Christmases past and arrange them in chronological order. Place them in an album and you'll have a wonderful collection of memories from years gone by. After Christmas this year, add your current pictures to the album to be enjoyed next season. Be sure to store this album with your Christmas decorations. The album will be extra-special because it is only brought out once a year, during the festive season.

★ *"We have a special Christmas photo album. It spans about 10 years and it is the only collection of family pictures that we have all in one album, from our first child's birth to the present. What a delight to see how the kids have grown and changed throughout the decade. It is fun to see some of their presents and what was special to them at the time. We enjoy seeing who we spent Christmas with, whether it was friends or relatives. Some of the relatives have now passed away which makes the album somewhat like a family 'history book'. The effort and time it took to put this collection of pictures together has really been worthwhile."* ★

Raising Kids...for the fun of it!

New Year! New Plans!

Take some time with your spouse to make plans for the upcoming year.   Book a sitter and go out to discuss your ideas.   What are your goals this year? Are there any areas of concern you'd like to address regarding your career, the house or your children? Perhaps you'd like to start a new hobby, sport or tackle a new job. To help get you focused during your 'planning evening', take along a note pad with a list of the following categories for you to consider:

- family/marriage
- vocation/career
- financial/material
- physical/health
- recreational
- social/community
- spiritual
- mental/intellectual

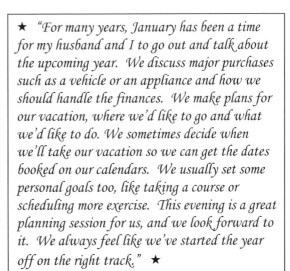

★ *"I was chatting with a friend who has older teenagers. She had realized that her family had missed the chance to go to Disneyland while their kids were little and she was really disappointed. After this discussion, I recognized that if we don't make formal plans, time just slips away and opportunities can be lost."* ★

★ *"For many years, January has been a time for my husband and I to go out and talk about the upcoming year. We discuss major purchases such as a vehicle or an appliance and how we should handle the finances. We make plans for our vacation, where we'd like to go and what we'd like to do. We sometimes decide when we'll take our vacation so we can get the dates booked on our calendars. We usually set some personal goals too, like taking a course or scheduling more exercise. This evening is a great planning session for us, and we look forward to it. We always feel like we've started the year off on the right track."* ★

Kid's Resolutions Too!

January is a good time to think about the upcoming year and also reflect on the past. Introduce your children to the process of setting goals or talk to them about making resolutions. Begin by asking a few questions to help get their ideas flowing. Do you have a personal goal that you'd like to pursue? Or is there a bad habit you'd like to improve? Discuss the possibilities or solutions with them, then try the following guidelines for implementing goals.

■ Begin with a few questions:

1. Is there anything about yourself that you would like to improve?
2. Is there something that isn't going smoothly at school, at home or with your friends?
3. Is there an activity you would like to try but haven't yet?

Your child's response will often lead to a discussion, or even a goal. For example your child might say *'I wish I wasn't late for school'.* A response like this easily leads to setting the goal of being on time for school this year.

> ★ *"My child has always been interested in art. When we discussed this year's goals for learning new skills and trying something different, we decided art lessons were a perfect fit."* ★

Possible resolutions or goals:
- be on time for school
- cut down on TV
- read more
- argue less
- keep room clean
- get more sleep
- hand in my homework on time
- practice piano nightly or learn to play a specific song
- learn to play an instrument
- start volunteering

■ Guidelines for Implementing Goals

1. **Set a goal.** Help your child determine a realistic goal.
   'I will be on time for school every day for the next two weeks.'

2. **Write down your goal.** Have your child write down their goal, sign and date the goal sheet.

3. **Brainstorm a plan.** Ask them if they have any ideas and work out a plan with your child to achieve their goal. Your child might suggest, *'I'll get up earlier'.* You can probe for more suggestions. *'That's a good idea, do you have any others?'* Listen to your child and implement their ideas where possible. Enourage them to do their own problem-solving, but be ready with other ways to help them be on time, such as:
   - lay out your school clothes the night before
   - place all homework in your backpack by the door
   - make lunch the evening before and have it ready in the fridge
   - get any field trip forms or other forms filled out and into your backpack

4. **Write out your plan.** You may want to include on their goal sheet some of the 'how to' ideas for implementing their goal. Decide where they could store their goal sheet.

5. **Implement your plan.** Provide encouragement when you see your child trying to achieve their goal.

6. **Adjust the plan.** Review your child's goal with them and adjust it where necessary. Younger children may need to use short-term goals that are daily or weekly.

7. **Celebrate success.** When your child has met their goal, acknowledge their achievement!

> *Encourage your child to place their goal sheet in a prominent spot like on their bedroom door or on the fridge. It will serve as a reminder and reinforce their commitment to their goal.*

Planning Ahead for Special Friends

Like most parents, do you notice how difficult it is to find time to socialize with your old friends or fit in visits with family friends? Try this strategy for reminding yourself to make that phone call and set up a date. Make a list of friends or families you would like to spend more time with. Write the name of one family at the top of each month on your calendar. As the year passes and you flip the pages of your calendar you will see their name. Take that gentle reminder and give them a call sometime during the month to set the date for a visit.

★ *"One January, my husband and I were reminiscing about some of the good times we'd had with friends. As we laughed over the stories, we realized how seldom we had seen some couples since our kids were born. We discussed how it was increasingly hard to keep in contact with many of our old friends. We realized that we needed a new approach for ensuring we got together with them over the year. We wrote the name of one couple on each month of our new calendar. The plan was to connect with them sometime in that particular month. Well, it worked for a whole year. We'd call up one couple per month and get together. The activities we planned ranged from a simple date where we'd have a coffee and a visit at our house, to going out to supper at a restaurant together. We even met one couple at the golf course for nine holes and had our visit during and after the game. Some of the get togethers with friends also included them bringing their children. These went especially well when their kids were close to the same age as ours. The plan to consciously reconnect with our friends really worked for us."* ★

Raising Kids...for the fun of it!

Family Fun

Fun Ideas That Won't Break the Bank

Check out these inexpensive entertainment ideas after Christmas, they're really easy on the wallet!

- **Have a candlelight family dinner.**

- **Free reading.** Go to the library; check out some neat books, magazines, music and movies.

- **Make Friday night your 'Games Night'.** Play charades, cards or board games.

> ★ *"A favourite activity in our home for years was 'puzzlemania'. We would build so many puzzles, including several big floor puzzles, that we'd fill up an entire room."* ★

- **Try 'Puzzlemania'.** Pull out all your old puzzles and start building. As you complete each puzzle, lay it out on the floor and keep building!

- **Have a comedy fest**. Have each person take a turn doing whatever it takes to make someone laugh.

- **Experience a new form of transportation.** Take a bus, subway or ferry.

- **Beat the winter blues, try an 'Indoor Picnic'.** Invite friends over for an indoor picnic, in the middle of winter! Spread a blanket out on your floor to sit on. Dine on rolled jam sandwiches, macaroni salad, carrot sticks and 'ants on a log' where you spread peanut butter on celery and place raisins (the ants) on top.

> ★ *"You should have seen the heads turn as vehicles drove by and saw our snowwoman in a bathing suit."* ★

- **Go tobogganing or ice skating.**

- **Play in the snow.** Bundle up and enjoy the white stuff:
  - Fill spray bottles with water and food colouring and create snow art.
  - Play in the snow using bowls and kitchen utensils.
  - Create whales, turtles or other animals in the snow.
  - Get out empty ice-cream pails, fill them with snow and pack the snow down well. Build a small fort or tower.
  - Make a snowman into a knight; use a garbage can lid as a shield and add a cardboard sword that's been covered in tinfoil.
  - Make a snowwoman; attach a two-piece swimsuit, add a sun hat and glasses.
  - Build a snowman, then fill a wagon full of snowballs and prop the handle against the snowman to make it look like he's pulling the wagon.
  - Dig out a snow cave from the pile of snow you have shoveled off the driveway.

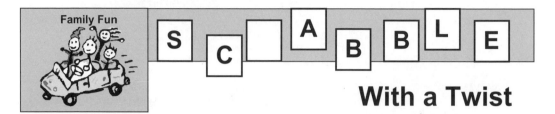

Family Fun

SCRABBLE

With a Twist

Gather your family together for a 'co-operative' game of scrabble. The object of the game is to work together as a team to reach the highest group score. Each player takes a turn using their own letters to form a word on the board, just like in a regular game of Scrabble. The 'twist', however, is in the scoring. Instead of individual scores, a running group score is kept. Every player contributes to the running total as they form a word and calculate the points for their word. Family members become motivated and excited to reach the highest TEAM score and *everyone* feels like a contributor.

Variation: Put a little friendly competition into your scrabble game by splitting the family into two teams. Be sure to make the teams as even as possible, for instance, one parent and one child per team. With small groups working together to form words, the younger kids will not only improve their spelling and increase their vocabulary, but will have a lot of fun too.

★ *"When our family played Scrabble, the younger two just couldn't compete for word scores with our oldest. They felt incapable or even 'dumb'. For many activities we believed competition is good—but this was not one of them; anyone feeling dumb wasn't a good thing. We tried to solve the problem by helping the younger ones to create words. This was okay, but they still weren't feeling like they were really contributing. Then we devised a scoring plan where everyone worked separately to build their own Scrabble words. Each person had ownership of their own words, but we kept score as a group. This simple solution made it fun for everyone."* ★

Raising Kids…for the fun of it!

Make A Date With Your Kid

Ever notice how your child reacts when you spend time alone with one of them? Without the phone ringing or other day-to-day distractions? Plan a date night with your child to really cultivate your relationship. Spend time together by simply going for a walk and talking or doing an activity your child likes. Invest time in your child, enjoy their company and build a strong relationship.

■ Ideas for fun things to do:

- Try something sporty:
  - mini golf
  - bowling
  - shoot some hoops at the neighbourhood playground
  - attend a sporting event
- Dress up and go out for dinner
- Head to a café for a hot chocolate or a latte
- Go to a live play, concert or musical theatre performance
- Visit a museum or art gallery

★ *"In an effort to create a closer relationship with my very private daughter, I tried to find some time alone with her. A tough fit for a working mom with two kids who are involved in a lot of activities. We soon realized our 'window of opportunity' was while my younger daughter was at her dance class. It was just enough time for us to shop together, go for a hot chocolate or browse through the bookstore. It was amazing how much she opened up, when it was just the two of us. Each week we both look forward to our special time together."* ★

It's a Beach Bash...

Check out these hot party ideas for a cold winter day. Create a great theme party with ideas for decorating, fun activities, food and drinks. Have everyone come dressed in beachwear or a grass skirt and then pretend you're on a tropical island.

★ *"I threw a beach party for my daughter, Andrea's, tenth birthday. The decorations were easy to come up with and the kids had a blast playing games and learning a Hawaiian dance. One little girl told me before she left that 'I didn't know you could have so much fun at a house party'. Another guest wore her grass skirt for Halloween the next year. This party left lasting memories for many youngsters and Andrea was thrilled that we went to all the effort for her."* ★

Invitations

Send a 'Message in a Bottle'. Place some sand in the bottom of a small glass pop bottle. Write or print out invitations on paper. Roll the invitation and put it just inside the bottle. Personally deliver the invitations to your guests.

I've discovered a terrific Hawaiian Island and would like you and a few friends to join me. If you find this note and can get to my island, on June 23 at 1:00 pm please call Andrea at 748-2456 to join the fun.

It would be great if you could wear a pair of shorts and a t-shirt or some Hawaiian clothes because the sun will be hot, hot, hot!!!

Make the paper look weathered by dipping the edges in tea and then lightly burning the edges of the paper.

Party Decorations

- Bring your patio lanterns inside the house and plug them in for the party.
- Arrange your lawn chairs and stand up beach umbrellas, then attach balloons to them.
- Blow up all your inflatable toys like beach balls, air mattresses and big shark or dolphin ride 'em toys and scatter them around the room.
  - Purchase netting from a hardware store and drape it over a curtain rod, stair rail or pictures.
  - Hang shells and plastic or cardboard fish, whales or dolphins on the walls or staircase.
  - Beach towels may be used to mark guest's chairs or place them in a big circle on the floor to laze around on, just like at the beach.
- Continue the theme with a blue or green tablecloth or a beach towel table runner.
- Decorate the table with an arrangement of seashells, coral and fish-shaped confetti.
- Use a small wading pool or an open cooler filled with ice to keep drinks cold.
- Make a sign to place on the wall above the food area to read 'Beach Corner Concession'.

> ★ *"Beach party decorations were so easy to pull together. I decorated the table with shells, some plastic fish shaped dishes, and served drinks with little umbrellas in sugar rimmed glasses. The kids were so impressed."* ★

Party Activities

Here are a host of fun things to do at the beach party. Select the activities based on the age of your guests; there are activities for younger guests through to the teen partiers.

■ 'Aloha!'
Welcome your guests by placing floral leis around their neck or grass skirts around their waist.

■ Read 'Rainbow Fish'

Read aloud this wonderful book by Marcus Pfister and then have some fun by creating paper fish. Use an oval paper plate as the fish. Glue on a tail, fish lips and an eye. Use non-toxic markers to colour the fish with polka dots, stripes or an abstract design. Brightly coloured tissue paper can be used for the fish scales or fins. Simply tear away crumpled pieces and glue onto the fish.

■ Cast-away Into a Fish Pond

Let the guests retrieve their loot bags with a fishing rod. Make a fishing rod by using a broom handle for the rod, a piece of thick string for the line and a clothespin as the hook. The weight of the clothespin will allow the string to travel through the air as each guest 'casts' towards the pond area. The pond area can be as simple as the sofa pulled out from the wall, or as elaborate as ocean waves shaped and cut out of a huge piece of cardboard that's been painted sea blue.

The birthday child or parent is positioned at the pond area and will either attach the clothespin to the loot bag, or if bag is too heavy, attach a paper fish with a given number on it. After guests 'reel in their catch', they will collect the corresponding numbered loot bag. Or let the guest 'cast' a few times, retrieving the contents of their loot bag attached to the clothespin, one piece at a time.

■ Take Home a Little Ocean

This cute 'ocean shaker jar' will have party guests grinning from ear to ear. To create one, simply add the ingredients and shake. Watch the sand and glitter swirl and settle creating a new scene each time. The kids can take their creations home as a keepsake from the party.

What you'll need:
- baby food jars
- ¼ cup water
- ¼ cup corn syrup
- glue gun & glue sticks

Ocean Shaker Jar

In a baby food jar mix equal parts of water and white corn syrup. Add glitter and your choice of accessories.

Secure the lid with a glue gun and let the guests shake up a tidal wave, watching the treasures settle again and again.

Accessory choices:
- glitter
- small shells
- costume jewels & pearls
- plastic fish
- aquarium gravel
- metallic confetti
- sand

★ *"She's had it for four years and yet my daughter still plays with her 'ocean jar' now and then. She loves to see everything swirl and settle into a different landscape each time she shakes it."* ★

Raising Kids…for the fun of it!

■ Make Grass Skirts

Grass skirts are fun to wear and they put everyone in the beach party mood. They can easily be made as a party activity using the following instructions:

<table>
<tr><td>

1. Fold one garbage bag in half width-wise.
2. Stitch or glue the bag together approximately 2" (5cm) from the fold line. This will create the casing for the waistband.
3. To make the 'grassy' part of the skirt, cut the lower portion of the bag into strips, up to one inch from the glue line.
4. Complete steps one to three for the second bag.
5. Thread the elastic through both waistbands to create a full gathered grass skirt.

</td><td>

What you'll need:
- 2 green garbage bags per skirt
- elastic approx. 1 yard (metre) per skirt
- cool melt glue gun or a sewing machine
- scissors
- plastic flowers or a floral lei

</td></tr>
</table>

6. Glue plastic flowers or a floral lei to the waistband.
7. The grass skirts are ready to be tied around the waist of your guests.

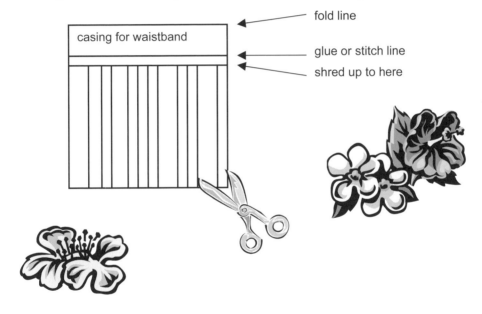

casing for waistband

fold line

glue or stitch line

shred up to here

Have a Beach Dance

There are many fun dances to have at a beach bash. So put on the tunes and follow the instructions for the limbo, Hawaiian Line Dance and musical towels. You'll also want to include some old dance favourites such as 'Surfing USA' by The Beach Boys, 'YMCA' by The Village People and 'The Bird Dance' by DJ Birdy.

Limbo Contest

Put on the song, 'Limbo Rock' by Chubby Checkers. This old song can be found at your public library or it can be downloaded off the internet. Do the limbo by holding a bar or broom stick and give everyone a turn to see how *low they can go* to get under the bar. The rule for the limbo is that you cannot touch the ground for support as you go under the bar. If you do you are given one more try. After two errors you are eliminated.

Musical Towels

Get each guest to spread out a towel on the floor. Start the music and have everyone dancing or moving among the towels. Stop the music and each person must find a towel to sit or stand on. The music begins again and one towel is removed. This time when the music stops everyone must find a towel, and therefore someone has to 'double-up'. No one is eliminated from play. As you continue to play and more towels are removed the task gets increasingly difficult. Eventually everyone is trying to fit on one towel—this is when the co-operation, creativity and laughter really come in!

Hawaiian 'Hang Loose' Line Dance

'Hang Loose'

Line dances are great fun to do at a party. The Hawaiian Line Dance is a simple one to learn because it primarily uses upper body movements and very little footwork. First, go through the steps and learn the dance without music. Each step is done to the count of four and therefore can easily be put to music afterwards. The 'Hang Loose' hand action is done by making a fist and then sticking out your thumb and little finger. Wiggle your hand, titling from side to side.

- Begin with the entire group facing the same direction and at least an arm's length apart. To accomplish this, have everyone hold their arms straight out to their sides and be sure they are not touching anyone else. If anyone is touching, have them move around as necessary, so that all dancers have their own space.

Raising Kids…for the fun of it!

Here are the steps for the Hawaiian Hang Loose Line Dance:

Step	Movements (with 4 counts in brackets)	Cue words for 4 counts when music is added
1	Wave right hand (1,2), wave left hand (3,4).	'wave, right, wave, left'
2	'Hang Loose' sign with your right hand (1,2). 'Hang Loose' sign with your left hand (3,4).	'hang, loose, hang, loose'
3	Roll arms in front as you bend slightly forward from the waist (1,2). Roll arms to the right as you bring body upright (3,4).	'roll, forward, roll, right'
4	Roll arms in front as you bend slightly forward (1,2). Roll arms to the left as you bring body upright (3,4).	'roll, forward, roll, left'
5	Right arm crosses over in front of body and pats the left hip twice (1,2), left arm crosses over top of the right and pats left hip twice (3,4).	'left, hip, right, hip'
6	Take right arm off left hip without moving the left arm and pat the right side of your bum twice (1,2), bring left arm to the left side of your bum and pat twice (3,4).	'right, bum, left, bum'
7	Pump both elbows back as you hop forward two times on both feet (1,2), hop as you make ¼ turn to the left while you clap twice shouting 'Hang Loose' (3,4).	'hop, two, hang, loose'
8	Repeat steps 1-7 facing the new direction.	

- Once you've learned the dance steps, a great song to use is 'Fun, Fun, Fun' by the Beach Boys. If you do not have this song, try any music with a strong peppy beat.
- Play the song and listen carefully to the beat before putting the line dance steps to music. Clap out the beat of the song so that you can get a *'feel for the music'*.
- Then, play the music again from the start and use the following cue words so the entire group begins the dance steps simultaneously, *'One, two, three and— wave, right, wave, left'*, and so on through to the end of the dance. Once you repeat all of the steps four times, you will be facing your original direction. Have fun and *'Hang Loose'*!

> ★ *"I had a group of older kids over for a party. I gave them the written instructions for the hang loose dance steps and told them to figure it out. What a riot to watch them!"* ★

■ Beach Ball Volleyball

Beach ball volleyball is a great way for the kids to burn off some energy and have fun. When you use a beach ball or a large balloon, it becomes an easy game to play. Players of any skill level can enjoy the fun.

Supplies and Equipment
- beach bucket or sand pail
- slips of paper with player's names written on them
- beach ball or large balloon
- volleyball or badminton net
  (If you don't have a net, lay a few chairs on their sides and drape them with beach towels or divide the playing court with a row of pylons or other markers.)

> ★ *"The kids didn't want to quit playing beach ball volleyball. They were jumping to reach for the balloon and really worked up a sweat. It was a great game."* ★

Pick the Teams
Split the group into two teams by picking names out of a beach bucket.

Court or Playing Area
Find a fairly open area to designate as the 'beach'. Split the area into two courts.

Object of the Game
Be the first team to reach 21 points.

The Play
Teams will go to their side of the court and you choose either team to begin the play. If team A is chosen to start, one player from the team serves the ball over the net to team B. To serve the ball, a player can either throw it over or volley it over the net. Team B then attempts to get the ball back over the net to team A. Teams can have up to 3 contacts or hits per side to get the ball over the net. The play continues with teams volleying or hitting the ball back and forth over the net until a team is unable to get the ball over the net before the ball lands on the floor. If the ball lands on team A's side, team B gets a point and the ball. Team B begins the next rally by tossing or volleying the ball over the net.

Variation: If teams are having trouble getting the ball over the net with a maximum of 3 contacts, you may change the rule to unlimited contacts per side.

Raising Kids…for the fun of it!

Beach Food & Beverage Ideas

A beach party theme is easy to continue with popular food items, utensils and drinks. .

■ Serve up some of these fun food ideas:

Go 'Kebob Crazy'
- Fruit Kebobs – cut a variety of fresh fruit into 1" cubes and place on skewers. Dole pineapple has fish-shaped pineapple pieces sold by the can that add a nice touch to the kebobs.
- Ham & Cheese Kebobs – skewer 1" cubes of ham and cheese onto cocktail picks and serve.

Tug Boat Treats
Place candies or nuts in new brightly coloured plastic tug boats.

Scoop Up A Snack
Use new plastic pails with shovels to serve snacks. Scoop out the snacks like pretzels, chips, nachos and cheezies onto individual serving plates.

> ★ *"The kids got a kick out of shovelling their snacks onto their plate."* ★

Veggies and Seafood
- Serve a shrimp ring with seafood sauce.
- Veggies and dip – fill the bottom half of a hollowed out red pepper with dip and place in the middle of a plate. Surround it with veggies.

Watermelon Fruit Salad
Use a hollowed out watermelon as a bowl, fill it full of fruit salad and serve.

Banana Split Mania
Put out the ice cream and toppings for a 'build-your-own banana split'.
Suggested toppings:
- strawberries – fresh or frozen in syrup
- bananas sliced length wise
- pineapple – crushed, canned or fresh
- chocolate and caramel toppings
- chopped nuts
- whipped cream
- maraschino cherries

■ Try out some of these cool drinks:

Tropical Drinks
Sugar coat the rims of the glasses by dipping in lemon juice and then in sugar. Pour the glass 1/3 full of cranberry juice and 2/3 full of ginger ale, garnish with little umbrellas or fruit skewers.

Mocktails
Older guests may like to mix their own 'mocktail' in a martini shaker. Try pineapple juice, sprite, a splash of grenadine and ice for a quick shaker mix. Or put out a variety of juices and pop for the kids to shake up their own creations. Be sure to serve the mocktails in martini or highball glasses, then top with ice, a marachino cherry or an orange wedge.

Party Favours by the Pail ━━━━━━━━━━━━━

Instead of using a treat bag, fill a plastic pail with party favours. Here are some ideas to choose from:

- inflatable beach ball
- glass floating fish
- fish fridge magnet or key chain
- shell or fish-shaped soap
- sunglasses
- candy – blue whales, gummy fish
- sunscreen in the sample size

Maximize Home Learning

Is your child constantly asking for homework help? Do you find yourself quickly making corrections to their work without actually discussing it? This is an easy trap to fall into, but doesn't necessarily help them learn. Your role is to guide and encourage your children through their homework rather than doing it for them. Encourage and help them to edit their own work rather than doing the editing for them. Identify areas that need improvement but have your child make their own corrections. Homework is assigned to extend their learning; use the following strategies to maximize your child's home learning.

Assist With Writing Skills

1. **Have your child complete the first edit.** Once they have completed their written assignment, ask them to read their work out loud to themselves and make corrections as they go along.

2. **Begin with some positive feedback.** After your child has done the first edit, read your child's work silently to yourself and point out to your child what you like about their work.
   Your first sentence really got my attention.
   You have used a lot of interesting ideas here.

3. **Identify punctuation errors.** Read your child's work out loud exactly the way they have punctuated it. Be careful not to pause or take a breath until you see a comma or period. Explain to them that a short pause in reading probably needs a comma. A long pause or new idea will require a period. A complete change in ideas requires a new paragraph. After you've done this with your child several times, they will be able to read their own work, noticing and correcting their punctuation errors.

4. **Identify errors rather than correct them.** This method forces your child to think about what is incorrect and then try to correct it on their own. This also helps to teach them how to 'self edit'.
   - **Circle the spelling errors.** Encourage your child to use a dictionary or spell check on the computer to make corrections.
   - **Circle letters that need capitalization.** Your child must determine why the letter is circled. Ultimately they will see that they have not capitalized a word.

- **Underline repetition of words in a paragraph such as 'that', 'this' or 'it' to show their frequency.** Suggest they replace 'it' with what 'it actually is' to improve clarity:

  When it was over she turned it off.
  When the movie was over, she turned the television off.

- **Encourage your child to use a variety of words and not to simply select a word because it's the easiest to spell.** Place a double underline beneath the easy words, to get them to think about using a better word.

  The big monster was scary.

  The gigantic monster was scary.

- **Check for clarity.** When reading your child's assignment, underline or place question marks by what is unclear and write in the margin 'unclear', 'explain' or 'tell me more'. Then verbally ask your child to tell you what they mean, or to explain it. Often when children describe their ideas out loud, it is easier for them to see where they need to add information for improved clarity.

5. **Talk with your child about adding detail to their writing.** Try one of these methods.

   - **Ask questions**. Who? What? Where? When? How?
     They drove in the red car.
     How did they drive? What kind of car did they drive?
     The boys drove cautiously in the shiny red convertible.

   - **Add interest to writing by using the senses**.
     How did it taste, feel, look, sound and smell?
     The flower was pretty.
     What did the flower smell like? What did it look like?
     The stunning red rose smelled sweet and its petals looked like velvet.

6. **Do a final read through.** Once your child has made all the changes to their work that you both felt were unclear, have them do a last read of their work to ensure nothing was missed.

7. **Give your child credit and praise for doing a good job.**

> ★ *"As a parent, I used to struggle with the kind of help I could give my child when they worked on their homework. I'm not a teacher, so it was often easier and seemed natural to just give them the answer when they asked a question. Then one day I picked up some great new tips while visiting a neighbour. When she helped her child with homework she didn't just give them the answer, instead she asked them such good questions and gave great feedback. She circled spelling errors and didn't just correct them. After seeing her in action, I was ready to try some new ways to help my kids learn more from their homework."* ★

Spelling Tips

Many children struggle with spelling. Here are a few easy techniques to assist your child with some commonly misspelled words.

1. **Say the word the way it is spelled and not the way it is pronounced.** Although it seems odd at first, this technique really works for spelling some difficult words.

Word	Pronounced	What to say to yourself in your mind when spelling
friend	frend	fri - end
tomorrow	tomorow	tom - or - row
answer	anser	an - swer
Wednesday	Wensday	Wed - nes - day
tarantula	teranchula	tar - an - tu - la
school	skool or scool	Sc - hool

★ *"I tell my kids when they are using the technique of saying the word the way it is spelled, to be very careful how they say it out loud. If they are in class and mistakenly say a word the way they spell it instead of how it is pronounced, such as fri-end, they'll get an awfully big laugh from their classmates."* ★

2. **Use acronyms.**
   If your child is having trouble spelling a word, make up an acronym to help them to remember. The goofier the acronym is, the more fun they will have and the more likely they are to remember it.
   Example:
   * because – **b**aby **e**ats **c**andied **a**pples **u**ntil **s**he **e**xplodes

3. **Find something in the word that can give you a little clue.**
    Example:
    *   Desert and dessert – these two are often misspelled.
        Desert is a dry sandy region; dessert is something you have
        after a meal. You always want seconds of de**ss**ert, this can
        help you remember dessert has two '**s**'s'. Or remember that
        the plural 'desserts' is 'stressed' spelled backwards.

4. **Dealing with homonyms.**
    Homonyms are words that sound the same but are spelled differently and have
    different meanings. Try to make a connection by looking for a smaller word within
    the word.
    Example:
    *   **Hear** – you hear with your **ear**. The spelling of 'hear' has ear in it.
        Here meaning a place, which is close to me and is in the word
        there, which is also a place.
    *   Princip**le** is a rule and has **le** in it, as does the word ru**le**.
        Princi**pal** is the one that runs a school and wants to be your **pal**.
    *   M**eat** has the word **eat** in it. You **eat** your m**eat**.
        Meet is in the word **meet**ing, where you meet.

5. **Learn to recognize spelling by sight.**
    Simply look at the word and see if it 'looks' properly spelled to you. Once you write
    out the word in one or two different ways, you can often pick the correct spelling.
    Example:
    *   bank or banc
    *   scissors or sissors

    > ★ *"When my daughter was young, she asked me how to spell the*
    > *word skip, 'is it spelled with a 'c' or ' k'?' I would respond by asking*
    > *her to write out both spellings. I found that with some words it's*
    > *very easy to recognize the correct spelling simply by seeing it."* ★

Raising Kids…for the fun of it!

Memorization

Check out the following rhymes, acronyms and other techniques to give their memory a boost.

■ Rhyming

- Encourage your child to remember the order of the planets in the solar system with this poem.

Mercury, Venus, Earth and Mars,
These are the planets among the stars.
Jupiter, Saturn, Uranus too,
Neptune and Pluto, I know them—do you?

- This is a tricky old rhyme to remember. Once it has been mastered, your child will always be able to remember the number of days in each month.

Thirty days hath September,
April, June and November.
All the rest have thirty-one,
Excepting February alone.
And that has twenty-eight days clear
and twenty-nine in each leap year.

■ Acronyms

Create words or sentences using the first letter of each item you need to memorize.

- To remember the Great Lakes think of the word **'HOMES'.**
  Huron, **O**ntario, **M**ichigan, **E**rie, **S**uperior
- Think of this statement to remember the order of the planets
  My **v**ery **e**xcellent **m**other **j**ust **s**erved **u**s **n**ine **p**izzas
  Mercury, **V**enus, **E**arth, **M**ars, **J**upiter, **S**aturn, **U**ranus, **N**eptune, **P**luto
- For the directions on a map, think clockwise '**N**ever **E**at **S**hredded **W**heat' for **N**orth, **E**ast, **S**outh, **W**est

■ Other Techniques

- **Count items in a list.** If your child has a list of items to remember, encourage them to count the items and then focus on the number. For example: it is easier to remember the names of the oceans if you know you need to remember six of them.

- **Repetition.** Sometimes there are no quick and easy ways to learn things, and a child may simply have to repeat the spelling of a word or a math formula to retain it. Have your child read it, say it and write it again and again to ensure it is solidly in their memory bank.

- **Recipe cards.** Use recipe cards when you have a lot of information to memorize, such as several difficult formulas, theories or history dates. Put one important piece of information on each card. Hole punch the top left hand corner of each card and put them all on a 1" (2.4 cm) ring or safety pin. Take the 'ring of information' wherever you go. Kids can go over as many facts as possible while being driven to a sports practice, while waiting in line at the grocery store or whenever they get a small window of time.

Study Group

Encourage your child to review or study with a friend. Set-up a specific time and choose a place. Provide a large table so they can spread out their notes. Suggest they review notes and ask each other questions. Encourage them to start their review with the areas that they didn't know very well. Perhaps their friend had a better understanding of that specific topic and could explain it in a way that made it clearer. Schedule the study group before each exam or as a regular weekly meeting. Serve healthy snacks for an energy boost.

> ★ *"My daughter was disappointed with her social studies test score and was asking me for help. We talked about starting a study group with a couple of friends who could meet each Monday after school for a couple of hours. I also suggested writing out the important dates and details after each social class on recipe cards so she could carry them in the car for review on the way to dance class. She was quite excited to try these new study techniques."* ★

Raising Kids...for the fun of it!

Enhanced Math Skills

If your child is having difficulty understanding an aspect of their math homework, it's best to help them as soon as possible. Math is one subject where skills are extremely cumulative, one builds upon another. For example, it is difficult to learn how to divide if your multiplication skills are poor. Below is a list of some ways to help your child with math homework.

■ Assisting with general math development:

- Suggest they look through their notes to see if there is a similar question that they've already completed.
- Use manipulatives, such as coins or Lego pieces for counting, addition, subtraction, multiplication and division.
- Give your child extra paper to write down all of the steps they took to answer the question, so you can determine where help is needed.
- Ask your child to say the steps out loud as they are doing them, this may make it easier to determine where the difficulty lies.
- If a question has many repeated steps, such as division, encourage your child to say the steps over and over again in their head. This will help them to retain the steps in their long-term memory.

■ Problem Solving

1. Ask your child to read the question out loud to you.
2. Ask your child to tell you in their own words what they think the question is asking.
3. Have your child underline key words or phrases in the question that give them clues as to what is being asked, i.e. the words *gave* or *took away* indicate subtraction.
4. Determine the correct or appropriate equation for the information given.
5. Solve the equation.
6. Write a full sentence answering the question. Be sure to have them check that their answer makes sense.
   Example:
   Tom has four more dollars than Jane. Jane has ten dollars and twenty-five cents. How much money does Tom have?
   To solve this equation you must add $4 to $10.25. 10.25 + 4 = X   X = $14.25
   Tom has $14.25, which is $4 more than Jane.
   If your child has mistakenly subtracted and gotten an answer of $6.25 ask them if it *makes sense.*

> *Encourage your child to ask questions in class, especially in math, because if they miss one single step, they could miss learning the entire lesson.*

Helping With Visual Projects

Equipped with the following series of questions, you can help your child to think through and take charge of their visual projects such as a diorama, model or a poster. It is so tempting to just jump in and get started assembling the project. But by starting off with a few important questions, your child will become more independent and able to tackle their next project on their own.

■ Prior to starting the project:

Get your child to read the assignment out loud to you. Have them highlight or circle the details such as the due date or marking criteria.
Begin with a few questions.

- Have you seen an example of the project?
- Do you understand the marking guide?
- What are your ideas for this project?
- How do you think that might work?
- How does that relate to your topic?
- What scene or diagram would you like to create?
- Where do you want to start?
- What materials do you need?
- Do we have all the materials you need for your project? If not, make a list of what you'll need and we'll shop for it.

■ When the project is finished, ask:

- What do you think of your finished project?
- Is there anything else you could do to make it better?
- How do you feel about the work you've done?

Raising Kids...for the fun of it!

Special Start to Valentine's Day

Not just a day for lovers, show your kids how much you care! On Valentine's morning, draw a heart or lips on the bathroom mirror with a felt tip marker before your kids get up, or greet them after their shower with a warmed towel or housecoat.

Sprinkle a few cinnamon hearts and leave a 'love-note' by their cereal bowl or tuck a few chocolate-kisses into their lunch kit. Then, wait and watch their reaction to these few simple displays of affection. The smiling faces will be worth all the effort.

By setting the tone for Valentine's Day, the mood could become contagious. Encourage your children to show their siblings and other family members how much they love and appreciate them. Make Grandma's day special with a quick phone call, or drop a valentine in the mail to Auntie. Today's the day to show you care—love is in the air!

Family Fun

Heart-warming Coupons

Make a coupon or two for someone special this Valentine's Day—or give them a whole booklet! Create the coupons on coloured paper using a computer, or by hand. Describe the service or product being provided. Include an expiry date to encourage prompt usage. Have fun with phrases or themes on the coupons. Decorate the coupons with clip art, drawings or stickers. Be sure to include hugs and kisses (XOXO) on each coupon.

Need a Ride?
Redeem this coupon
for 1 round trip,
Love Mom and Dad   OXOX
Expires Nov 30

★ *"One Valentine's Day I was thrilled to receive a coupon book full of promises, redeemable upon request. My daughter felt such pride presenting a gift she made all on her own. She promised to deliver the services whenever I asked. She learned first-hand that the value of the gift is not related to the amount of money it cost, instead that a gift from the heart is priceless."* ★

Coupons for Children

♥ **Fun Afternoon Together** – Cash this coupon in for a fun afternoon together playing ball or monopoly or reading stories – it's your choice.

♥ **Be the King (Queen) for the Morning** – You'll be treated royally by your loyal servants (your parents!). Your special morning begins with breakfast in bed, followed by your choice of TV shows until noon.

> **A picture says it all.**
> Include a drawing, sticker or clip art on coupons for young children that can't read. They'll understand the contents of the coupon at a glance.

♥ **Home-made Cookies** – Exchange this coupon for a batch of home-made chocolate chip, oatmeal raisin or peanut butter cookies.

♥ **Got Soccer on the Brain?** Exchange this coupon for a family soccer match.

♥ **Safari Adventure** – Trade this coupon for a family visit to the zoo.

♥ **Reading Rampage** – Redeem this coupon for an outing to the library.

♥ **Go Fly a Kite** – Trade in this coupon for a trip to the park on a windy day to fly a kite with Mom or Dad.

♥ **Candy Store Visit** – Trade this coupon for a dollar's worth of candy treats.

♥ **Ice-Cream Delight** – Cash in this coupon on a hot day to get an ice-cream treat after school with Mom or Dad

♥ **Lace up Those Skates!** This coupon entitles you to an hour's skate at the neighbourhood rink.

♥ **Take a Journey into the Past** – Trade this coupon for a trip to the museum.

Coupons Teens Will Love

♥ **Shoot Some Hoops** – Redeem this coupon for a game with Mom or Dad.

♥ **You're the Winner!** You get to pick the rental movie and your parents cover the cost.

- **Need Pampering?** Redeem this coupon for a special spa bath, complete with a couple of candles burning around the tub, scented soaps and lotion and a nice warm fluffy towel.

- **Room Service** – This coupon entitles you to one free 'clean up' of your room. Mom or Dad will pickup, do the dusting and vacuum for you.
- **Movie Night** – This coupon entitles the bearer to admission at a movie of your choice. You can take along a friend!
- **A-Golfing We Will Go** – This coupon entitles you to a free game of mini-golf or a bucket of balls at the driving range.
- **Snack Attack** – This coupon can be cashed in for a tray of nachos for you and a friend.
- **Need a Ride?** This coupon entitles you and a friend to one round-trip taxi ride provided by Mom or Dad.
- **CD or Book** – Cash in this coupon for a new CD or book.
- **Nails Done by Mom** – Trade this coupon for an at-home manicure or pedicure, complete with massage and nails painted by Mom.
- **Decisions, Decisions** – This coupon entitles you to choose the fast food restaurant, redeemable the next time Mom asks, 'Where should we go?'
- **Shopping Anyone?** – Exchange this coupon to go window-shopping with Mom or Dad.
- **Great View** – That's right, cash in this coupon for the privilege of riding in the front seat for one round trip.
- **Speedy Laundry Service** – Trade this coupon for one load of laundry done on short notice – no questions asked!
- **There is Such a Thing as a 'Free Lunch'** – Redeem this coupon for the privilege of having Mom pack your lunch today, or spring for cafeteria fare.
- **Café Cruise** – This coupon permits you to a cruise down Main Street to a nice café, slip in for a special tea or hot chocolate, compliments of Mom or Dad.

★ *"When my son turned 13, I wanted to give him a gift that acknowledged him entering his teen years. I made up a coupon book full of special privileges. One coupon promised that he could stay up as late as he wanted on a chosen evening – no questions asked. Another one allowed him to watch an entire NHL hockey game without either of his brothers changing the channel. His favourite coupon was the 'Get out of Jail Free' coupon that he tucked away to use when he really needed it. Some of the coupons were for fairly normal activities, but because they were written down and given as a 'privilege' – it made them special. As he opened the gift and read the contents of each coupon out loud to the family he really got it! Being a teen was going to be great."* ★

Coupons to Give Grandparents

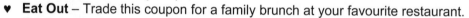

- ♥ **Hankering for a Visit?** You got it – just cash in this coupon. You pick the day and the whole family is coming over for a visit.
- ♥ **Church Service** – Remember when we were young and we all went to church together? Present this coupon and we'll pick you up and go to church with you.
- ♥ **Wild Wild Weeds** – Present this coupon for free weeding service for a section of the garden or flowerbeds.
- ♥ **Helping Hand** – This coupon entitles you to an 'Odd Job' afternoon – we'll complete a few household chores for you or with you – you name the date!
- ♥ **Movie Night** – This coupons entitles you to an evening together with all of us. We'll bring an old favourite movie such as 'Gone with the Wind' or 'Fiddler on the Roof', your pick.
- ♥ **Eat Out** – Trade this coupon for a family brunch at your favourite restaurant.
- ♥ **Feelin' Lucky?** This coupon can be traded for a games night to play scrabble, crib or charades.

Remember The Love of Your Life

- ♥ **Who's in control?** This coupon entitles you to total control of the remote control for one evening of television viewing – without a single disapproving glance from me!
- ♥ **Rub-a-Dub** – Trade this coupon for one free exterior car wash and interior vacuum.
- ♥ **Surf's Up** – Cash in this coupon for one hour of free surfing the web, even if you have chores waiting. Use it wisely!
- ♥ **Stressed?** Trade this coupon for a relaxing massage, (by me, of course). Guaranteed to soothe away the stresses of the day.
- ♥ **Room Service** – This coupon entitles the bearer to their favourite breakfast in bed.
- ♥ **Get out of Jail FREE Card** – This coupon entitles the bearer to one free 'goof up', without word said from me!!
- ♥ **Put your feet up** – Redeem this coupon for one afternoon of no yard work – watch from the sidelines 'sipping a cold one' while the family does the job!
- ♥ **Maid Service** – This coupon entitles you to a night off…no dishes tonight, no housework, no errands or chores. I've got you covered!

> ★ *"Last Valentine's Day we told our kids the story about how we met, our first date together, and where we went on our honeymoon. We brought out the pictures and had fun retelling some romantic memories. The kids loved hearing the stories and it even rekindled a little flame between my husband and I as we recalled those wonderful times we'd shared."* ★

Spring

St. Pa-TRICKS

Add a little zing to March 17th! Play leprechaun tricks and find a treasure. Or have fun while you eat your 'greens' all day long. Go ahead—try something new this year!

Leprechaun Tricks

Play a few tricks around the house before the kids get up to make it look like a mischievious leprechaun has been by.

- **Write a special message on a mirror or window.** Use green eyeliner or a green white-board marker, to write *'Happy St. Patty's Day'*.
- **Set your table with green napkins or a green tablecloth.**
- **Use Lucky Charms cereal.** Generously sprinkle Lucky Charms all around on the table like confetti.
- **Tint the milk in the fridge green.** Add a few drops of food colouring to the milk in the fridge and the kids will enjoy the surprise as the milk pours out.
- **Play Irish music.** Find music by 'The Irish Rovers', or a good selection is *'When Irish Eyes are Smiling'*.
- **Make leprechaun flowers.** Place a few white carnations in a clear vase; add water and lots of green food colouring. Over a few days, the green water travels up the stem and through the flowers to tint the white carnations green. Your children will be amazed by this leprechaun trick and learn all about osmosis too.

> ★ *"Just before breakfast, my son went to the fridge to pour himself a glass of milk. Lo and behold...out of the carton came green-tinted milk! The look of surprise on his face was hilarious. 'A leprechaun must have been in our house!' I responded. He excitedly called to the rest of the family to come and see what had happened. I smiled to myself and thought how clever I was. It was sure an easy trick for such a great reaction."* ★

The luck of the Irish to ya' on St.Patty's Day!

> Purchase miniature shamrock stickers to place on your kids' cheeks or fingernails. Or try a washable tattoo pen to draw St. Patrick's Day designs.

Catch a Leprechaun

Perhaps, with a wee bit of Irish luck on March 17th your kids could catch a leprechaun in a trap. Try this unique little idea for St. Patrick's Day and *tickle your kids with some Irish fun.*

A couple of days before St. Patrick's Day, help your children build a trap for the leprechauns. Dig a hole in the ground and camouflage it with branches and twigs. Or if you have snow on the ground, dig a big hole in the snow and conceal the opening by laying a large white sheet over top. To entice leprechauns, which are sure to be passing by this time of year, sprinkle shiny items on the ground around the trap like glitter, tinsel or tinfoil. Once the kids have gone to bed on the night before St. Patrick's Day, secretly slip a little treasure inside the trap. Then next morning, have the kids check the trap to see if a real leprechaun has fallen into their clutches. There may not be a leprechaun, but they'll be happy to find the treasure.

> ★ *"Riley and Sam decided to build a trap to try and catch a leprechaun. They dug a hole in the snow in the backyard and sprinkled bright coins all around. The next morning, the boys went out to inspect the trap. They were disappointed that there wasn't a leprechaun caught inside. But their disappointment turned to delight at the sight of small green footprints up the inside wall of the hole, and especially at the treasure left inside. News of the leprechaun trap spread throughout our neighbourhood and the next year new designs turned up in several different yards."* ★

■ Leprechaun Treasure

Leprechaun treasure can include treats that are sweet or shiny, and especially ones that are green. Plastic zippered sandwich bags are great to hold any loose candy that the leprechauns have supposedly left behind.

Green Candy Treats
- Peppermint gum
- Gummie frogs
- Aero mint chocolate bars
- Ring pops
- M& M's
- Smarties

- Sour soothers
- Alien pops
- Suckers
- Spearmint leaves
- Jelly beans
- Jujubes

Other Treasure
- Pennies or coins
- Gold coin chocolates

Raising Kids…for the fun of it!

Eat Your 'Greens' all Day

■ 'Greens' for Breakfast

Serve up some green pancakes. Use your favourite pancake mix and add some green food colouring. Serve with sliced kiwi, honeydew melon or green grapes. For a beverage, pour some milk to see if a leprechaun has been by—*'Green milk anyone?'*

■ 'Greens' for Lunch

Wrap ham around a pickle and roll it up inside a spinach tortilla shell. Dip celery, zucchini, broccoli, and cucumber in green dill dip. Accompany with key-lime yogurt. For dessert, indulge in some of the green candy from the leprechaun treasure.

■ 'Green Up' St. Patty's Dinner

Guacamole & tortilla chips
Spinach pasta with pesto sauce
Creamed chicken with peas
Lime juice & ginger ale
Frozen lime sherbet

Create a Leprechaun
Ask your children if they've ever seen a leprechaun and then get them to create one for you. Gather all the necessary materials; paper, pencils and crayons or modeling clay to create 3-D leprechauns. They'll have fun, and you'll all be surprised at the imaginative creatures they've made.

Rainy Day Activities

It's raining and you've got a case of the 'blues'? Turn any rainy day into a fun time with these great indoor activities.

Fun and Games

- **Make a fort with blankets and chairs.** After the kids have built their fort, stock it with books, toys and games. Take in a reading light or a flashlight to help you see so you can *play the day away.*
- **Assemble kits received as gifts.** Get out the models, craft kits or birdhouses that you've received for gifts and haven't had the time to make.
- **Snuggle up in the biggest bed and read.** Settle in and take turns reading a story out loud together. Or each have your own book to enjoy and read alone.
- **Teach your kids to juggle** (or have them teach you).
- **Take a trip down 'memory lane'.** Dig out old photo albums or watch family videos.
- **Make a batch of play dough.** Now watch kids of all ages enjoy molding 3D creations.

- **Work on a jigsaw puzzle.** Set up the card table by the fireplace or a comfy spot in your house and start working on a jigsaw puzzle.
- **Go to a craft store.** Let the kids pick out a project.
- **Write a story together.** Choose a setting for your story and have each family member create a character. Next, decide the story line and what problem has to be solved. Talk about solutions and then make a plan. Younger children can be the illustrators, while older children can compose the story and use the computer to write it out.

> ★ *"Instead of being disappointed on a rainy day, we'd pull out the blankets and chairs and start building a fort. A great spot was next to the sofa which gave us extra support for the frame of the fort. Once built, we'd cuddle up inside and read books together. Then the kids would play for hours on their own."* ★

Word Puzzles

■ Get Warmed Up and Solve Some Puzzles

1.	Wear Long	6.	Man Board
2.	Stand I	7.	Dice Dice
3.	Mind Matter	8.	Ecnalg
4.	0 —— M.D. M.S. Ph.D	9.	R I A T S
5.	Death Life	10.	Knee Lights

Answers:
1. long underwear
2. I understand
3. mind over matter
4. 3 degrees below 0
5. life after death
6. man overboard
7. pair of dice
8. glance backwards
9. upstairs
10. neon lights

■ Create Your Own Word Puzzles

One way to help your kids make their own word puzzles is to have them think of a word or phrase that includes either an action or a shape. Then they can design a visual that will represent the word. Examples:

Downtown – make town go down

    T
    O
    W
    N

Around the World – draw a circle around world

Sandbox – make a box around sand

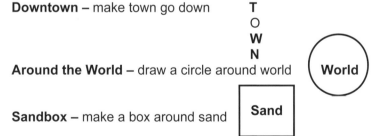

■ Exchange the Word Puzzles

Take the word puzzles that everyone has designed and swap them among all of the participants. Try to solve each other's 'brainteasers'.

Kids' Craft Box

Stock up a craft box with *'precious items'* for your kids.
Collect items like empty paper towel rolls and egg cartons.
In addition to the 'used stuff' you collect, add newer materials,
such as construction paper in a variety of sizes and colours, felt pens, crayons, and
glue. Now everything they need to build their creations will be available in one location.
On a rainy day or just *any* day, bring out the 'Craft Box' and let your children use their
imaginations! If they need a bit of guidance, give them a suggestion of what to build
such as an alien, a home for their favourite stuffed animal, a landing strip and airport for
their toy airplane, or a decoration for Grandma's fridge.

Recycled items for a craft box:
- scraps of coloured paper, wrapping paper
- empty paper towel or toilet paper rolls
- netting from garlic or onions
- egg cartons
- plastic fruit baskets
- scraps of lace, faux fur
- buttons
- fake jewels
- interesting parts from old toys
- old fridge magnets
- used calendars
- pictures out of old magazines
- small boxes from items bought or received
- springs and wires
- string

★ *"My son never tires of creating things out of the stuff in his craft box. There are many times when I walk into his room after a lazy Saturday afternoon spent all by himself or after a play date with a friend, and the 'junk' is strewn all over. There are creations galore made out of almost anything. In fact, now I hardly ever put an item in our recycle bin, I simply clean it off and add it to his craft box."* ★

Family Fun

Terrific Fun in a Tickle Trunk

Girls and boys love to play make-believe, especially dressed as their favourite character, princess, knight or spy kid.

Create a 'tickle trunk' full of clothes, costume pieces and accessories. Collect party dresses, tops with glitter and sequence, fur pieces, hats, wigs, jewellery and glasses. Be sure to include a blazer, tie, old sports uniforms, construction hat, lab coat, and any character costumes that you have.

Purchase affordable and unique items for your tickle trunk from:
- *dollar stores*
- *second-hand stores*
- *garage sales*

Accessories for your trunk:
- fake glasses, nose, moustache
- glasses with googly eyes
- sheriff's badge
- pirate hat and eye patch
- wand
- crown and tiara
- magnifying glass
- hats and scarves
- shoes and purses
- jewellery
- long gloves
- veil
- belts and ties
- medical kit

★ *"Our tickle trunk was the most popular in the neighbourhood. The girls had dresses, jewellery and accessories for many identities. They could dress up as a princess in my old bridesmaid's dress that I had modified by adding elastic around the neck. The big floppy hat and glitter scarf completed the 'ensemble'. Or the lab coat and tie turned the neighbour's kid into a Doctor, especially when he added a medical kit. Countless hours were spent in make believe places because of the great pieces in our tickle trunk."* ★

★ *"My thirteen year old son brought home a group of friends to work on a skit for his Language Arts class. He had volunteered our house since we had such a great selection of articles in our tickle trunk. I had thought of selling the trunk and its contents in our garage sale last summer—good thing I didn't!"* ★

A Slumber Party to Remember!

Do you have fond memories of a special sleepover from your childhood? With pillow fights, games, and giggling till the wee hours of the morning? Here's a party you can host that will be equally memorable. Included are a variety of activities to ensure great fun and laughs. Choose ideas from the list that you think would suit your guests or modify them for any age group of either boys or girls.

Invitations

Create an invitation with a 'night time' theme and decorate it with glow-in-the-dark stickers and glitter. Using black card stock or construction paper, write *'Come to my Slumber Party'* across the front of the invitation. Then sprinkle white stars and moons randomly across it. Use gel pens to write the party details inside, including the date, time and place. Be sure to include the morning pick-up time, as well. The gel pens *glow* on the black background. Have fun with initials, **B.Y.O.P.P.S.B.** (**B**ring **Y**our **O**wn **P**ajamas, **P**illow, and **S**leeping **B**ag).

Party Decorations

■ Wall Decorations

Continue with the 'night-time' theme as you decorate the house. Make stars and moons out of cardboard and cover them in tin foil or decorative gift-wrap. Use clear thread or fishing line to suspend them from the ceiling. As an alternative, you can spray-paint the moon and star shapes. Use sticky tack to attach decorations to the wall.

> Some party supply stores sell large cardboard stars that can easily be used for decorating.

■ Table Decorations

Spread out a white or yellow paper tablecloth on your table and write 'Happy Birthday' across it in big letters. Bring out a bunch of crayons or markers and let the guests 'doodle' and write messages all over it. This is ideal at a sleepover because the kids have plenty of time to hang out and create a design.

> ★ *"I knew the kids would enjoy doodling, they started as soon as the pizzas were in the oven. What I didn't anticipate, was how many times they'd come back to the table and add details. It was great fun."* ★

Food Ideas

■ 'Build-Your-Own' Pizza

Purchase individual pizza crusts or make some of your own. Provide a variety of prepared toppings such as ham, pepperoni, salami, mushrooms, mozzarella and Parmesan cheese, pineapple tidbits and fresh tomatoes. Let the kids assemble their own selection of toppings and then bake the pizzas in the oven. Be sure to mark the pizzas in some way to ensure that each guest receives the one that they actually put together.

> *Tip: Consider limiting the amount of pop and sweet treats as it gets closer to bedtime. Some children will have difficulty getting to sleep if they have too much sugar.*

■ Birthday Cake

A yellow star-shaped cake is an easy and effective way to extend the party theme. Put a happy face on the cake and use charcoal-coloured icing to apply an outline that will emphasize the star shape.

Crafts

■ Personalized Bookmarks

Have guests create their own bookmarks. Allow ample time to do the artwork and to really 'personalize' them. Encourage the kids to draw pictures of their favourite hobby, sport or other interests. Once completed, laminate with iron-on plastic. Hole punch at the top and run a ribbon or tassel through the hole.

You'll need:
- thick card stock paper, cut into pieces 1.5" x 6" (4 cm x 15 cm)
- a variety of felts and pencil crayons
- glow-in-the-dark stickers
- plastic iron-on laminate
- special hole punches, such as stars or hearts
- ribbon or tassels

■ Sleeping Bag Covers

Purchase plain inexpensive fabric and sew simple, oversized pillowcases. Make them large enough to be used as a sleeping bag cover. If sewing is not an option, you can buy ready-made large white pillowcases. Thread a ribbon or some cord through the hem to be used as a drawstring closure. Let the guests use fabric paint to decorate the covers and to write their name for easy identification.

You'll need:
- fabric or one large pillow case per person
- ribbon or cord
- fabric paint in a variety of colours

Games and Activities

■ Makeovers

Girls enjoy doing beauty makeovers of their hair, nails and face. Purchase individual hair accessories, lip gloss and a few mini-bottles of nail polish from the dollar store for this activity. Ask them to bring along their own make-up if you'd like to include a face make-over as well. Arrange to have a video camera so that you can film the entire event. The girls can watch the video later in the evening and have a giggle at the results.

> If possible, have a digital or Polaroid camera on hand to take 'before' and 'after' pictures. Send them home in the loot bag for each guest to have as a keepsake.

> ★ *"By the amount of laughter coming from the bedroom where this activity took place, I'd say it was pretty successful!"* ★

■ Play 'Secret-Secret'

Ideas for 'Secrets'
Tongue-twisters:
'She sells sea shells by the sea shore.'
'Eunice is used to shopping in unique New York.'
Phrases that are reversed:
'The sky is green and the grass is blue.'
Silly rhymes:
'Sleepovers are fun, we laugh, we cry. But no sleep—Oh why? Oh why?'

Prior to the party, write silly sentences or rhymes on slips of paper that the kids can take turns pulling out of a hat. To play 'Secret-Secret', have everyone sit in a circle and then choose a person to start the game. This person pulls a 'secret' from the hat and reads it privately to themselves. They turn to the person sitting on their left, and whisper it into their ear. That person turns to the next player in line and whispers the phrase that they have just heard. This continues around in the circle until everyone has had a turn.

The rule is that each person can only whisper the secret once. If the recipient doesn't hear it very well, they simply repeat what they *thought* they heard. This is where the fun actually comes in. The last person says the 'secret' out loud. It's fun to see how different the story is by the time it reaches the last child. Now begin again by having a different child take a secret from the hat, be sure everyone gets a turn. Then have the kids create their own phrases, sentences or short stories to pass around the circle. Now you'll really hear the chuckles!

Raising Kids…for the fun of it!

■ Play 'Bucketball'

Bucketball is both fun and easy to play, which makes it a great activity for burning off excess energy at your child's slumber party.

Court or Playing Area
It can be played either indoors or out.

- Indoors – When playing indoors, the court is determined by the size of the room you are using. Because the space is limited indoors, everyone must play on their knees to keep the movement restricted.
- Outdoors – Outdoors the court is marked with pylons or other objects. Players are able to stand up to play since there is ample room to move around.

Equipment
- 2 containers of equal size, such as ice-cream pails or cardboard boxes
- medium-sized soft nerf ball or some sort of s*quishy* ball.

Game Set-up
- Pull names out of a hat to make 2 teams. Flip a coin to see who gets the ball first.
- The game begins with all players standing anywhere on their own 'half' of the court, except for goal catchers who are positioned on opposite ends. Once the first pass is made, players are allowed to go anywhere on either side of the court to play.

The Object of the Game
The object of the game is to pass the ball from one player to another and shoot it towards your goal catcher, who is standing at the opposite end of the court. The goal catcher tries to catch it in their bucket or container, which scores a point. Game ends either once a certain time limit is reached or after a specified number of points is scored.

The Play
Whoever wins the toss gets possession of the ball at centre court. If it is team A, they pass the ball from one player to another down the court and try to score. Once a goal is scored, play begins again as it did at the start of the game, with all players on their own half. The team that was scored upon, in this case team B, is given the ball at the centre. Team B now attempts to pass the ball down their court and score a point. Either team can intercept a pass at any time, giving them possession of the ball and they can work together to try to score. Other bucketball rules include:

- Players must pass the ball to move it down the playing area; they cannot dribble or run with the ball.
- Players cannot have possession of the ball for more than 5 seconds at a time.
- There is no physical contact, e.g. pushing or elbowing.

If there is a violation of any rule, the ball is given to the opposite team.

■ Play 'Consequences'

Get ready for lots of giggles with this game of silly stories. Give everyone a pen and a blank piece of paper. The paper must be thick enough so that you cannot see the writing through it. The game starts with each person writing a female's name at the top of their paper, such as a TV or movie star, friend or a teacher. The paper is then folded over so that the name cannot be seen and the paper is passed to the guest on the right, who fills in the next portion of the story. This person **must not look** at what was written underneath as they write '*and* _____' (the name of any male). Once again, the paper is folded and passed to the right. It continues in this fashion until the entire wacky story is written. Again, secrecy is critical. All the steps to the story are outlined below:

Leader reads out loud:	Guests write: (example only)
Write the name of a female.	Lucy
Write 'and', then the name of a male. (Encourage names that most guests will know)	and Jim
Write 'met at' and the name of a place.	met in the drama room at school.
Write 'he said' and then write something he said.	He said, 'Let's go play ball.'
Write 'she said' and then something she said.	She said, 'I want cheesecake.'
Write an action sentence. e.g. They went…. or He took her to….	He threw her in the air and tried to catch her, but missed!
Write the name of another person, try using someone older and more mature.	Mr. Graham
Write 'said' and then what that person said about the incident.	said, 'That sure was a great world series!'

Note: This example is for the reader's use only, specifically to help understand how the game goes. Do not read everything to the guests; let them discover how the stories get all mixed-up.

Once everyone is finished, open up the folded stories and take turns reading the amusing results out loud together!

★ *"My kids loved playing 'consequences' so much that we played it for two years in a row at their birthday parties. Once they've all had a turn reading the crazy stories, everyone usually begs to play another round. In the second round their stories get even more outrageous."* ★

Raising Kids…for the fun of it!

■ Let's dance!

Spot Dances
Secretly pick a special spot on the floor or the ceiling before the music begins. Start the music and encourage the dancers to move around the dance floor. Stop the music and

the person closest to the spot that you chose, wins a prize.

Variation: Once the music is stopped, give your guests several directions, such as: *'Move 2 steps forward, 3 steps to your left, 5 steps backwards, turn 3 full turns to your right, and 4 steps forward.'* The person who has moved closest to the chosen spot wins a prize.

Pass the Pillow
While the music is playing, a pillow is passed from person to person all around the dance floor. When the music stops, the person holding the pillow gets one point against them. Continue for several songs, where the object of the game is to have the fewest points.

Bunny Hop
Use the song 'Locomotion' for the Bunny Hop. The entire dance is done with participants lined up behind one another in a long line. Each dancer connects to the person in front of them by holding onto their waist or their shoulders. The object is to stay in the line and try not to come apart while you do the dance steps together.

> **Possible prizes:**
> • candy, bag of chips or chocolate bar
> • a magazine or a book
> • a neat candle

The steps for the Bunny Hop include: kick right, kick right, kick left, kick left, hop forward, pause one beat, hop backward, pause one beat, hop forward three times, and continue to repeat the steps above until the song is over. Use the following prompts to help get everyone moving forward in unison: *'ready, and...right, right, left, left, forward, pause, back, pause, 1, 2, 3.'*

Other Dances
Try other dances that your guests may be familiar with, such as the Macarena or Electric Slide, the Schottische or Butterfly.

> ★ *"The girls didn't want to stop dancing. One of them led the rest of the group in a line dance called the 'Macarena'. A couple of the girls didn't know the dance before they came to the party, but they definitely knew it after they danced the same steps to four songs in a row!"* ★

■ Play 'Flashlight Tag'

In this game of tag, the person who is 'it' has the flashlight; all other players are hiding randomly in the dark. Once the flashlight shines on a person who is hidden, they must run quickly to get out of the light. The person who is 'it' chases and tries to tag them, with the help of the flashlight's beam. If tagged, that player becomes 'it' and is given the flashlight to help them catch one of the other players.

■ Play 'Hide and Seek'

Purchase one flashlight or glow stick per child. Include one in each loot bag at the end of the party.

Use mini flashlights or glow sticks in a darkened area of the house or yard to play hide and seek.

★ *"Playing games outside in the dark is enticing. We could hardly get the boys back in the house to have snacks and do some other activities."* ★

■ Tell Ghost Stories

Older children enjoy telling ghost stories in the dark using only the light of a flashlight. The kids can either make the stories up or you can have some on hand so that everyone can take turns reading. Look in your local library for a collection of spooky short stories.

Raising Kids…for the fun of it!

Gift Opening

Play a combination of 'Spin the Bottle' and 'Truth or Dare'. Have all guests sit in a circle on the floor. The birthday child places the bottle on its side in the middle of the circle and spins it. When it stops spinning, determine who the neck of the bottle is pointing towards. The birthday child will ask that person the first question, *'Do you want truth or dare?'* If the guest says *'truth'*, the birthday child asks them a question that they must answer truthfully, such as, *'Who is your favourite boy in our class?'* If the guest says *'dare'*, the birthday child must choose an activity to dare them to do, such as *'I dare you to stand on your head,'* or *'I dare you to turn in a circle 3 times with your eyes closed, and then take 4 steps forward'*. Once the guest has completed the truth or dare directions, they will give their gift to the birthday child to open. After the gift is opened, the bottle is then spun again to determine who goes next.

Loot Bags

Send home the items you have purchased for each guest:
- flashlight or glow stick
- hair accessories, lip gloss or nail polish

Include any items you have made:
- bookmark
- pillow case/sleeping bag cover
- digital or Polaroid makeover picture

Other:
- bubble gum
- comic book
- a can of Coke or Pepsi (to keep them awake on the day after the party)

Breakfast

By now you're probably exhausted, so keep breakfast simple with muffins, bagels, fruit, and juice, which are easily prepared. Or get more elaborate with pancakes, whipped cream and sliced strawberries. Blend up some fruit shakes to enjoy.

★ *"We have had some awesome birthday parties through the years, but my daughter's favourite would have to be her slumber party when she turned ten. We played a lot of activities and Bucketball was a real hit. Then there were the sillier games where we laughed all night long. Her friends, who are now 14, still talk about that party. And often when someone comes for a sleepover, they'll bring their sleeping bag to our house in the decorated cover we made four years ago."* ★

Kids Got Spring Fever?

The days are getting longer. Are you finding it hard to keep the kids to their scheduled bedtimes with the sun shining so bright? Even if your child can't go to sleep, encourage them to go to bed and read…or at least have some quiet time and rest.

★ *"It was spring time and we were having trouble getting our children to bed on time; we were constantly nagging them and we knew this had to change. My husband and I decided that getting to bed on time was the responsibility of our 10 and 12 year olds, not us. We explained to them that from now on, if they got to bed late, there would be a half-hour penalty effective the very next night. For example if they did not make it to bed by 9:30 p.m. on Monday, then on Tuesday they would have to be in their rooms by 9:00 sharp – a half-hour earlier and NO exceptions. Now that the issue was addressed as a family, the kids knew we were serious. In order for this situation to improve, we realized that we'd have to monitor the consequence closely. It only took one night when the boys had to be in bed by 9:00 instead of their regular 9:30. The next evening, they watched the clock themselves to be sure they were in bed on time and avoid the penalty. After that they needed a few reminders, but bedtime went much smoother and it made our children accountable, not us!"* ★

Focus on Learning

Keeping the Focus

We're on the 'home stretch' of the school year, how can we keep our kids focused? One great strategy is to write down year-end goals—when the March or April report card arrives, it is the perfect opportunity. Have your children review their report card comments and their grades, then give them a few days to think about their goals for the final reporting period. Check to see if there are specific comments in their report card, such as 'weak in their times tables', or 'needs to use more descriptive words in his writing'. If so, you can use the comments to provide a starting point for goal setting.

■ Choose a Specific Goal and Make a Plan

Goals must be specific, with an action that is measurable and a time-line attached. If a goal is 'specific', then the child knows exactly *what* is expected of them and by *when*. A major benefit of using specific goals is that success is easily seen.

- **Non-specific goal** *'I will improve my times tables.'*
- **Specific goal (include the 'how?')** *'My goal is to do 40 times tables correctly in 2 minutes. To reach this goal, I will do multiplication flashcards 10 minutes a day all term. I'll do 'mad minutes' two times per week to increase my speed.*

■ Maintain the Goal

Once the goal is attained, help your child decide how they can maintain it.
Example:
'Once I reach my goal, to maintain my multiplication skills I will continue to do mad minutes on Tuesday and Thursdays.'

* 'Mad minutes' are when a specified number of math questions are to be done in a pre-determined time. To choose the amount of time to allot, make sure it is challenging but not discouraging. As your child improves over time, increase the number of math facts, increase the difficulty or reduce the time allotted.

★ *"My daughter was having difficulty with her addition facts in grade two. First I had her make flashcards, which gave her practice with her calculations. She wrote the equations on the front of a card in pen or a dark colour and the answers on the back lightly with pencil. This way she couldn't see the answer when looking at the front of the flashcard. To help her, I made up a 'mad minutes' sheet on our computer. I started with 15 easy questions, where each number was five or less, e.g. 4 + 2 = __. 5 + 3 = __. I gave her one minute to answer the 15 questions. In her first attempt, she got 14/15, so we increased the number of questions to 20 in order to push her to do the calculations more quickly. Over time she mastered this; we then went to 30 questions, and so on. Once she mastered 40 questions in two minutes, we increased the difficulty of the questions, by adding higher numbers, e.g. 5 + 6 = __. 7 + 7 = ___. Her skills and her confidence grew in leaps and bounds."* ★

Celebration Plate

Has your child just learned to tie their shoelaces, finished reading their first chapter book, played at recess with a new kid in class or babysat for the first time? As a parent, it is sometimes difficult to find ways to honour or congratulate your children when they make you proud. Beyond a pat on the back or a trip for an ice cream, try serving them dinner on the 'celebration plate'. The next time you are shopping, purchase a plate that stands out or looks different from your regular dinnerware, for instance, a bright yellow plate with big flowers on it. When the occasion arises, set the table and give this special plate to someone who deserves recognition.

★ *"The following heartfelt letter accompanied a 'red plate' that my family received from dear friends."* ★

Dearest Friends,

We wish to share with you a unique and traditional part of our family. The gift is a simple red plate. However, in our home, the 'red plate' means a lot. We use it to symbolize the little joys, simple celebrations and milestones that come our way. Be it a birthday, an anniversary, an exceptional accomplishment, a special guest, a surprise act of love, a random act of kindness, or an overwhelming chore completed…there are so many reasons to celebrate our families.

In our home, the 'honoured person' uses the 'red plate' at dinner or breakfast or whenever.

We've given this plate to you with hopes that your new red plate will be used often and with good cheer. May it brighten someone's day or honour a friend, and become a tradition in your home as it has in ours.

Wishing you much love,
Lorrain, Roger, Simone, & Max

'Let's Talk…and talk and talk and talk!'

Communication is the foundation of any good relationship. Discussion and conversation are vital if you want to connect with your kids, build strong family bonds and then maintain them. So just talk with them. Talk and talk and talk and talk. Talk about school, about their friends. Talk to kids about their feelings, help them put into words how a situation 'feels' in the pit of their stomach. Reassure them that it is okay to feel afraid or upset or sad. And listen. Really listen to what they have to say, face-to-face. Give them your undivided attention. And then, share your thoughts and your feelings with them. Give a little piece of yourself to them, open up. If you talk with your kids about yourself and relate your experiences and how you felt, it will help them to talk openly about themselves. Keep the communication lines open, through the elementary years and far into the teen years.

Why Talk?

Why talk? There are so many reasons to talk with your kids.

- **The sheer enjoyment of conversation.** Have fun chatting and enjoying each other's company.
- **Really get to know your kids.** What are their feelings, their reactions, their likes and dislikes? What do they dream about and wish for? Be 'in-sync' with each other and really get to know one another. If you think about it, isn't that how you get to know your friends and business acquaintances—by having conversations with them and learning about them, by investing time in a relationship? Why not try that same method with your kids?
- **To keep yourself informed.** Find out information about their day and their life —what they learned in school, how things went at recess, about their teacher and their friends. Keep informed about homework and how they are doing in school. Be aware of their challenges and struggles in school or at recess. And remember to point out their strengths and successes as well.

> ★ *"When I ask my kids about their day, I always ask what they did at recess or at lunch break. Their interactions with their peers outside of the classroom are as important as how they did, for instance, on a math test."* ★

> ★ *"Sometimes I make a point of asking, 'What was the best part of your day?' or 'What did you do really well in at school today?' I try to focus on the positive and not just on their challenges or the negative."* ★

- **Problem Solve.** Discussion can help kids learn how to handle situations as they arise, from conflict at the playground as a youngster to your teenager reacting to a fellow junior high peer. What is an appropriate or positive way to handle a situation…'*Let's talk about it.*' Discuss other possible ways they could have handled it. Remember to discuss your issues at work occasionally too; your kids will see different ways to cope with a problem and ultimately how to solve it.

  They also learn that it is normal to have difficulties between people that need to be resolved.
- **Learn the 'art of communication'.** By talking with your kids, you teach them an invaluable life skill—how to carry on a conversation. They need guidance and experience to learn how to communicate appropriately in a variety of settings. Encourage your kids not only to answer questions, but to reply and then to ask a question in return. When an adult asks a child how they are, it is okay to respond with '*good*' or '*fine*' but teach them to reciprocate with, 'And how are you?' This is one step to communication. Kids need to learn how to ask questions and to show interest in others—their parents, relatives, and their peers.

★ *"When we're gathered around the dinner table and discussing the day's events, I might say, 'Did anyone ask Dad how his day went?' I want to teach my kids to include everyone in the conversation. Our family conversations often focus on the kids, and I want them to see that we also need to take the time to focus on others, in this case—their parents."* ★

When to talk?

There are many good opportunities to have a discussion with your child. Prime times for conversations are:
- **Walking or driving home from school.** A great time to strike up a conversation is right after school when their experiences are fresh in their mind.
- **Around the table at mealtime.** Turn off the TV—mealtime is the perfect opportunity for good conversation. Everyone is finished their day's work and it is time to reflect on areas of interest or to discuss issues that may have arisen through the day.
- **During 'drive time'.** Whether you are off to an activity with the kids, running errands, on a vacation or any other time you are driving—it's the perfect opportunity for discussion. There are very few distractions like TV, siblings, or the phone ringing. Ultimately, you have a captive audience—your child can't walk away or ignore the conversation.
- **At Bedtime.** Some kids really open up when it's time to go to bed. It may be the only time in the day that your child gets one-on-one time with a parent.

> ★ *"I'll often bring up the difficult topics when we are in a vehicle. It seems it is easier to discuss the tough stuff when we are both looking ahead and not face-to-face."* ★

Raising Kids…for the fun of it!

How to talk?

There are many ways to strike up a conversation.

- **Ask a variety of questions.** One excellent tip is to have a variety of ways to initiate a conversation. If you always ask the kids, *How was your day?* it is pretty easy to answer with a one word answer like, *Fine* or *Okay*. Try a different question like:
    - *How did the math test go?*
    - *Did you start any new units today?*
    - *What did you do in gym class?*

Here are some other questions you can ask, specifically to learn about their class and classmates at school:
    - *Who's the class clown?*
    - *Who puts up their hand the most often to answer questions?*
    - *Who is the best worker?*
    - *Did you have any class discussions in any of your subjects today?*
    - *What was it about and what was your opinion in the discussion?*
    - *Name one thing you learned today that you didn't know yesterday.*

- **Indirectly bring up a topic.** A very effective way to begin a conversation is by referring to an outside source. Casually bring up topics like:
    - *My friend at work was telling me about her daughter…*
    - *I read an article in the newspaper…*
    - *I heard about…*
    - *I saw…*

★ *"I have found the 'indirect' approach to addressing certain topics with my kids seems to really work. For instance, if I want to discuss chores—to say that we aren't happy with the way the kids are doing chores in our house will get a negative reaction right from the start. But if I begin the conversation by saying, 'I was talking with my friend today and their family has a neat way of sharing the work at home.' Talking about someone else seems to take the edge off. The kids don't feel threatened in any way and everyone is more likely to listen and give their input or reaction."* ★

- **Use role playing and discussions.** Discussion or role-playing is effective, especially when you are dealing with character development. For example:

Fairness	– What would do you do if someone doesn't let you play with them at recess?
	– What words would you use or should you just ignore them? Let's try that right now.
Honesty	– What would you do if your friend wants to borrow your answers for a Math assignment? They are clearly cheating, but are you cheating too, by giving it to them?
	– How would you handle it?

- **Conversation starters.** Write up some questions on small pieces of paper. Place them in an envelope that can be kept handy in the kitchen. Pull one out to place in the centre of the kitchen table occasionally at meal time. Make the topics interesting:
  - What is your favourite TV show and why?
  - Which cartoon character are you most like? Least like?
  - Which character do you like the least and why?
  - Who is your favourite teacher and why? What about your least favourite?
  - Who is your best friend? What traits does a best friend have?
  - Who is your mentor?

Or use some more serious topics.
  - What if your friend lied to you and you found out?
  - What would you do if someone offered you drugs?

- **Newspaper clippings.** Cut out an important article from the paper and read it out loud for everyone to discuss.

- **Parents sharing their own stories.** Sharing stories about your experiences as a child will help give your kids ideas on how to deal with difficult issues.

> ★ *"Our family was chatting in the living room one night and we started telling stories about embarrassing moments we'd each had. As we told the stories, we were able to laugh about situations that were once quite upsetting and embarrassing. My husband told us how embarrassed he was years ago when he asked a girl out for a date and she said 'No'. He described how 'crushed' he was and how he really didn't know what to say back to her. It was a great opportunity for a discussion about how that might feel. It was definitely 'food for thought' for my two kids in their early teens, since they could soon be facing similar situations. This conversation had us considering how to say 'no' in a kind way, as well as thinking about how to handle a rejection."* ★

What about difficult topics?

Topics like sexuality, drugs, and STD's are very difficult to discuss. If you ignore these topics completely, you'll be relying on the media, friends and teachers to educate or inform your kids. This is probably not wise. Use any of the techniques listed above to introduce a topic, perhaps a newspaper article can break the ice or bring up the topic indirectly by *'On the news I saw…'*, or *'A friend of mine told me about…'* One very important point is to talk about crucial issues while they are young. You, as a parent, are the main source of information when they are young and they trust and believe what you have to say. Once kids hit the teen years their parents are no longer the 'experts' they once were, your child's peers and the media are a bigger source of information.

★ *"One day I began a conversation with my son in grade 7, 'I understand you've started the human sexuality unit in health class and that you're learning about safe sex. (pause) You know, when you decide to be intimate with someone—now, I realize that won't be until you are probably in your twenties, but…' My son listened to my advice even though it really wasn't relevant to him at this point. But he did take in the information and I hoped he'd remember it if and when he found himself in a situation where he needed it. Having the same conversation with my older teenager, I could tell she almost tuned me out completely. I realized too late, that I had missed the 'prime' opportunity for this discussion with her. I was upset about this until I read an article in a parent's magazine. It reassured us that even if your teen doesn't appear to be listening—they are and to keep talking to them, especially about such important issues."* ★

★ *"A friend of mine is a police officer. She told me about the importance of talking to my kids early about drugs. So one night when our boys were aged 10 and 12 years old, my husband and I spoke with them. We asked what they knew about drugs and then we exchanged all kinds of information. We discussed how certain drugs are illegal in our country and if they were caught using them, they would have a criminal record. Sure the record would be removed when they turned 18 because of the Young Offender's Act, but the information would always remain in their file. Was it really something they wanted on file—the repercussions of a poor decision would be with them forever. We also talked about and role-played what to do if they were at a party and some kids were doing drugs, or offering them drugs or alcohol. We told our boys to remove themselves from the situation by saying something like, 'I need to get something out of my car.' Or 'I have to make a phone call.' Or 'I need to use the washroom.' And then leave. We assured them that no matter where they were or what time it was, that we would always come and get them. We were glad we had this conversation while they were young. It has kept the door open to talking about drugs as they have entered their teen years."* ★

Family Fun

Pull a Prank—It's April Fool's Day!

When was the last time you got away with playing a prank? Well, take advantage of April Fool's Day—it's your perfect chance! Here's a few to pull on your kids; they're sure to get a reaction from someone in your family.

- Stuff the toes of your kid's shoes with tissue.
- Remove shoelaces and hide them in their jacket pocket.
- Hang their jacket *inside-out* on the hanger.
- Put a plastic spider under the breakfast table.
- Give your child a fake phone message, '*Sara called and wants you to call her back.*' When your child returns Sara's call and asks her what she wanted, you intervene with, '*April Fools!*'

> *Remember that April Fool's only lasts until noon on April 1st. Play your trick early, before 12:00, or you will be the 'fool'.*

- Take a pen apart and put an April Fool's message inside. When the pen will not work and they take it apart to find the problem, they'll see your silly note.
- Put salt in the sugar jar. Who will get salty coffee or cereal for breakfast?
- Ask a question or shout out a sentence where you get a quick reaction:
  Look at the bunny in the backyard.
  What's that red mark on your shirt?
  or *Look-out behind you!*
  Once you get a reaction just follow up with, '*April Fools!*'

The riskier the prank, the bigger the laugh and the more memorable it will be. So—go for it!

- Yell *'Fire!'* When everyone comes running to investigate, wait a moment or two, then simply say '*April Fools*'.
- Call your husband and tell him you're pregnant!
- Call a neighbour to say you've fallen and you think you've broken something.

> ***WARNING! WARNING! WARNING!***
> *Recipients of April Fool's pranks usually 'get even'.*
> ***Be on the look out!***

Raising Kids…for the fun of it!

★ *"One year we were on vacation during Spring Break. As I was relaxing around the pool, I realized I had lost track of time and that it was the first day of April. It was close to noon, so I didn't have much time to play an 'April Fools' prank. My husband was inside in the lounge area of the hotel, enjoying a baseball game on TV. I was playing in the pool with our boys. Parker, our youngest, was four at the time and still required a lot of supervision. I thought to myself, here was my chance. I simply opened the door to the lounge area and yelled, 'Garry, come quickly!' He jumped up and raced frantically to the pool knocking over anything in his path. Once he got to the pool, I said, 'April Fools'! We all laughed, but in Garry's momentary fear and shock, he picked me up and sent me flying into the pool. This is one of the best April Fools stories our family tells each year. I got into a little trouble that year, but it was worth the fun family memory."* ★

Family Fun

Mealtime Madness

Need a little laugh at dinner tonight? Try something out-of-the-ordinary…

■ Backwards Dinner – 'Dessert first, please!'

Have a little fun with your family at dinner tonight. Explain to everyone that they must come to the table wearing their clothing backwards, including shirts, pants, hats, belts, sweaters, vests or glasses. 'Backwards Dinner' begins with dessert, followed by the main course and finishes up with an appetizer. This dinner is a blast anytime, but would especially suit April Fool's Day.

■ 'Dig-In' Dinner

Tonight at dinner, serve the meal but don't set out any of the usual utensils. Instead, as they come to dinner, hand out some wild 'n crazy utensils like a potato masher, soup ladle, ice-cream scoop or spatula. Once seated, have the family 'dig in'!

★ *"We arrived home for dinner one day and it seemed like everyone was a little cranky. Just for fun, as we all sat down to the table, I handed out silly utensils from the kitchen drawer like an oversized fork, a whisk, and an ice-cream scoop. The entire mood changed instantly—have you ever tried to eat spaghetti with a whisk?"* ★

Hippity, Hoppity, Easter's on its way…

'Here comes Peter Cottontail, hopping down the bunny trail…'
Greet your guests this Easter with a display at your door or a window scene of bunnies and eggs. Two simple, but effective ideas are found below.

■ Easter Display

Create a simple Easter display of bunnies and other young spring animals such as chicks or lambs. Get the kids to take a good look around the house; you'll be surprised at what they'll find that is just right for a 'spring' or 'Easter' theme. Gather stuffed animals, figurines or even pictures of animals that you enjoy. The display can also include Easter baskets, painted eggs, or symbols from the Easter Bible Story, such as a cross or palm branch. Arrange your display at a focal point visible from your front door for everyone to enjoy.

■ Paint up a Window Scene

Spread Easter cheer by painting your windows with bunnies, eggs and baskets. Try this easy to use paint mix: 1 tablespoon (15 ml) of dish soap
                        ½ tablespoon (7 ml) of tempura paint powder
Water colour paints will also do the job, or you can create a more translucent window design by using white-board markers.

> Use masking tape to protect the caulking on the window. If any paint or ink from the marker comes in contact with the caulking, it could permanently discolour.

> ★ *"We had a lot of fun painting our windows one year. We used a colouring book and followed the simple outlines. It was so easy to draw a bunny or a fancy Easter egg using the pictures as a guide. As the Easter season drew near, every single visitor that came by commented on our window art and the kids smiled. Following the pictures in the colouring book was easy and it made us feel like real artists."* ★

Family Fun

Create Old-fashioned Easter Eggs

Decorating Easter eggs is a tradition that can bring the whole family together, from preschoolers to grandparents. Virtually everyone will delight in their Easter egg creations. A big part of the fun is finding a variety of ways to decorate the eggs. We've included several neat ideas, sure to inspire you!

Decorative Eggs You Can Keep

Hollowed eggs are very fragile making them more difficult to decorate than hard-boiled eggs. However, the advantage of decorating hollowed eggs is that you can keep your 'creations' for several years.

How to hollow eggs:
1. Puncture both ends of the egg with a long needle; be sure to pierce right through the yolk.
2. Make one hole larger than the other, so it will be easier to blow the 'insides' out.
3. Place a short straw over the smaller hole to blow until the egg is hollow inside.
4. Rinse the hollowed egg with warm water, allow it to dry and it's ready to decorate.

Decorative Eggs for One Season

Hard-boiled eggs are easy to decorate because they are not as fragile as hollow ones. However, the disadvantage is that your decorated eggs *cannot* be kept past the Easter season. Here's a method to boil eggs that ensures flawless eggs without a crack, which will colour beautifully. This is an alternative to hard-boiling an egg by bringing it to a 'full boil', which makes the eggs more susceptible to breaking or cracking.

How to make 'perfect' boiled eggs:
1. Place eggs in a cooking pot and cover with cold water.
2. Bring to a boil and as soon as the water is boiling, shut off the heat source.
3. Leave the pot on the same burner for one full hour and drain.
4. Immerse eggs in cold water for 30 minutes to cool. Drain and allow them to dry; they are ready to decorate.

Mix Up the Colours

Decide which colours you want to use on the eggs. A typical package of food colouring has the four primary colours: red, yellow, blue and green. Follow the package directions to mix additional colours, such as orange or purple.

Before colouring eggs, lay a large old towel on top of your working space. It will absorb spills quickly, so your table will not be damaged by the dye solution.

To prepare each individual colour, you'll need:

2 cup	plastic/glass container	500 mL
½ cup	vinegar	125 mL
½ cup	hot boiling water	125 mL
20 drops	food colouring	

Put vinegar and hot water in a container. Add approximately 20 drops of food colouring, or until desired colour is reached.

And Decorate

■ Personalized Eggs

Kids really enjoy seeing a decorated Easter egg with their name on it. Extend this idea to adults as well. Make 'personalized eggs' for all your Easter guests and then use them to mark the spot where each person will sit for Sunday dinner.

1. Use a white wax crayon to write your name on an egg.
2. Draw shapes and designs around your name, such as a zig-zag lines and diamond shapes. Add a simple picture of one of your favourite things, such as a basketball, flute, or teddy bear.

You'll need:
- white wax crayon
- variation:
  coloured crayons

3. Place the egg on a teaspoon and carefully immerse it in coloured water of your choice. Dip it several times until the desired depth of colour is reached. The result is a coloured egg with white markings, personalized especially for you.

Variation: Use coloured wax crayons to do your artwork.

★ *"My youngest daughter chose her first egg carefully and wrote her name on it with white wax crayon. She then drew a few hearts and stars on the egg. When she dunked the egg in and out of the coloured water, the eggshell quickly absorbed the beautiful blue colour while the water simply rolled off the wax markings. Her eyes lit up as her drawings and her name seemed to magically appear. The designs she'd drawn were a vivid white colour on the bright blue background, they were gorgeous! What a great start to her Easter egg decorating."* ★

Raising Kids…for the fun of it!

■ Tie-dyed Eggs

Most people are familiar with tie-dyed t-shirts. Here you can help your child use a similar method to decorate eggs.

1. First choose a background colour for your egg:
   - If you choose a plain white egg, it will give you a bright white background, and ultimately more contrast in the finished product.
   - If you choose to lightly tint the egg to begin with, it gives a more subtle tie-dyed effect. To create a light background colour, simply dip the egg a few times in the colour of your choice.

> **You'll need:**
> - thin cotton cloth or facial tissues
> - eyedropper

2. Wrap a thin cotton cloth tightly around the egg.
3. Using an eyedropper, drip a variety of colours randomly on the cloth.
4. Keep the cloth on the egg for a few minutes to allow the colours to soak through the cloth onto the egg.
5. Unwrap to see your creation. The egg will have absorbed the multi-colours, creating a funky tie-dyed effect.

> ★ *"Tie-dyed eggs are my son's favourite to make. He wraps up his egg and then carefully picks the perfect places to drip the different colours. The next step is always the hardest as he waits for a few minutes while the colour is absorbed by the shell. He can hardly resist peaking under the cloth. The best part is taking the cloth off to see the neat designs."* ★

■ Half & Half Eggs

> **You'll need:**
> - an egg holder

This is a very simple technique that is great for young kids. The 'two-toned' design looks neat lying in a basket alongside the other decorated eggs.

1. Dip one-half of an egg in one colour and then let it dry completely on an egg stand.
2. Next, dip the other half into a different colour for a two-toned effect.

■ Marbled Eggs

> **You'll need:**
> - vegetable oil

This technique leaves a marbled effect on the eggs and the oil gives the eggs a lovely shiny finish.

1. Dribble different colours of dye from your food colouring package into a container and add some vegetable oil. DO NOT STIR.
2. Dip an egg quickly in and out of the container to develop a 'marbled effect'. Dip it several times until you have the desired intensity of colour.

■ Candle-waxed Eggs

Dripping candle wax on an egg gives it a unique 3-dimensional design.
1. Place egg in an 'egg holder' to keep it stable.
2. Use a variety of coloured candles to drip wax in an abstract design all over one end of the egg. Let the wax harden and repeat on the other end. This results in an interesting waxed design.

You'll need:
- pastel-coloured birthday candles
- matches
- egg holder

★ *"I like the eggs that are decorated with candle wax the very best. The look is unique and they capture everyone's attention."* ★

Variation 1:
After the wax on the egg dries, dip it in a coloured mixture. This will color the white areas not covered by the wax.

Variation 2:
Take an egg that has already been 'marbled' or 'tie-dyed' and add the wax drippings.

■ Polka-dot Eggs

These polka-dotted eggs are the most difficult to make, your kids will need patience and a steady hand. The hard work pays off when the technique is mastered, they'll have a distinctive egg design.

You'll need:
- small candle
- matches

1. Create a light background colour on an egg by dipping it a few times in a coloured mixture of your choice. Let the egg dry thoroughly.
2. Light a small candle and carefully drip small wax circles or ovals onto the egg, randomly or in a specific design. If you keep the wick short, it will help to make small precise drips.
3. Once the wax is completely dry, dip the egg either in the same coloured-solution, which will make it a darker shade of the original colour, or dip it in a completely different colour to create more contrast. Be sure the second colour is quite intense.
4. Let the egg dry thoroughly once more, then carefully peel the wax off to reveal a beautiful polka-dot design.

★ *"A lot of people asked my son how he made the egg with light pink polka dots on the bright green background. It's an eye catcher."* ★

Variation: For a 3-D effect, leave the wax on the egg.

Have fun decorating eggs. Use the methods described alone, or mix up some of the techniques. Let your imagination go! Display the beautifully decorated eggs together on a plate or in a shallow basket for everyone to enjoy.

Raising Kids…for the fun of it!

Family Fun

Easter Basket Treasure Hunt

Here's a neat way to hide the Easter baskets this year. Use a treasure hunt where the story is presumably told by the Easter Bunny himself. Simply write the clues on some bright paper and hide them around the house. Keep clue #1 to read out loud to your kids as they begin the hunt and hide clue #2 by the toothbrushes, clue #3 in the carrot bin and so on.

Clue #1 – read out loud to the kids	#1 'The Easter Bunny has big teeth that he likes to keep really clean.'
Clue #2 – by the toothbrushes	#2 'I need to eat these orange vegetables to keep me healthy.'
Clue #3 – in the carrot bin	#3 'I love good music, do you have any rabbit songs?'
Clue #4 – by the stereo	#4 'My toes are so cold; I hope you don't mind that I borrowed some socks.'
Clue #5 – in the sock drawer	#5 'I like orange juice for breakfast, do you?'
Clue #6 – on the juice jug in the fridge	#6 'Do you watch cartoons?'
Clue #7 – by the TV	#7 'Bunny ears need to keep warm in the winter. Can I use your toque?'
Clue #8 – with hat & mitts	#8 'Hey, have you baked any Easter cookies this year?'
Clue #9 – in oven	#9 'I just learned to ride a bike last year; can you show me yours?'
Clue #10 – outside, by bike	#10 'I've been busy all morning; I think it's time for a snooze.'

The Treasure – an Easter basket hidden in your kid's bed!

A Dynamite Detective Party

Get all the clues for a Detective Party that would intrigue even Sherlock Holmes! Entertain your detectives-in-training with activities where they solve mysteries using their investigative skills. This party will thrill the most inquisitive youngsters and be remembered and talked about for years.

Invitations

Set the stage for activities and games at this top secret party with a witty invitation like the one featured here:

Calling all Detectives  **It's Jordan's Birthday!**	We want you for a top-secret mission! Your great skills of investigation are requested. Your assignment begins: At _____ On _____ Time _____ The chief detective will provide food and gear, but you must confirm your acceptance of this mission by calling Agent "99" at: 436-5555

> **Ask guests to come dressed in spy attire…** *a parent's plaid blazer or a trench coat and hat.*

Variation: An invitation for the younger crowd.

I spy someone turning 7

Decorations

Make large muddy footprints leading up the walkway to the front door. Cover the door with a full sized poster, *'Detectives ONLY'* to give the appearance of an exclusive meeting place. Hang a 'Keep Out' sign on the door handle.

The mystery and intrigue continues inside the house, where gigantic question marks are hung on the walls, along with enlarged black fingerprints. Place a black tablecloth on the dining room table. Play a Pink Panther or James Bond soundtrack as the party guests arrive.

> ★ *"We hosted our son's detective party at his Dad's office. When we got there, a 'Detectives ONLY' sign was found taped on the door to the back entry. We told the guests that we had to use the 'secret' entrance to the building. We climbed the stairs to the conference room where several chairs were positioned around a table. On the white board was written, 'Welcome Detectives'. We told the guests to have a seat and we could get the secret meeting started. As they all sat down on the big office chairs, my husband and I smiled at each other—the scene had been set perfectly!"* ★

Loot Bags (a.k.a. detective kits)

On arrival at the party, each guest receives their own specially marked detective kit in a manila envelope. Detective's names are written on the envelopes along with *'TOP SECRET'* and *'CONFIDENTIAL'*. Use the contents of the loot bags during the activities at the detective party.

Loot Bag Contents
- a small mirror, or magnifying glass
- a disguise like a fake mustache or a 'Groucho Marx' nose with glasses
- gum
- 'detective' note pad: a brown top-coiled note pad
- pencil, pen or invisible ink and decoder pen
- detective badge

Games and Activities

■ Welcoming Activity – Which Detective Am I?

Prior to the party ask your child to list names of detectives that they know. Use your child's list to make nametags. The nametags are made from 2" x 3" (5 cm x 8 cm) card stock or paper. As guests arrive, tape a mystery detective name on to the back of each guest and the birthday child too. This allows players to see everyone's name, except their own.

Detective Names
Sherlock Holmes
Watson
Maxwell Smart
Agent 99
Pink Panther
Inspector Poirot
Scoobie Doo
Shaggy
Fred
Velma
Dick Tracy
Roger Rabbit
Frank and Joe Hardy
Nancy Drew
Carmen San Diego
Harriet the Spy
James Bond

Now let the fun begin. The detectives must question each other in order to guess their mystery identity. You must give them very clear instructions as to which type of questions they are allowed to ask. They may only ask questions that require a 'yes' or 'no' answer, such as:

> Am I a woman?
> Do I have a partner?
> Am I a cartoon?

They cannot ask questions that require more than a 'yes' or 'no' answer, such as:

> Am I a man or a woman?
> Which movie did I star in?

FINGER PRINT POWDER

Once detectives have asked enough questions to determine their mystery identity, they take the nametag off their back and place it on the front of their shirt, for everyone to see. Extend this idea during the rest of the party by referring to each child by their 'detective name'.

★ *"We've used the 'Who Am I?' game for many birthday parties. For our Detective Party we used detective names. One year we had an 'All Sports Party' and during the meal, we taped the names of famous athletes on the guests' back. As they ate, the kids tried to figure out their new identity. If a guest has a good sense of humour, just for fun I will tape a female name on a male's back, or vice-versa. The funniest one that our whole family remembers is when we were having a Disney theme party and I taped 'Tinkerbell' on Dad's back—it was worth a laugh!"* ★

■ Guessing Game

Before the party, cover a medium-sized box with wrapping paper, newspaper or brown paper and mark it 'TOP SECRET'. Cut two round holes on opposite ends of the box, one for each hand to fit through. Place 8-10 small items into the box, such as a key, a candle, ball, pen, paper, glove, mini magnifying glass, string, paper clip, eraser, toy car. To begin the game, give each agent a paper and pen and introduce the activity by, '*We will now test your investigative skills*'. Get each child to feel the items in the box, and then pass the box on to the next player. Give a 1-2 minute time limit per child, to secretly write down all the items they can detect.

You'll need:
- a medium-sized box
- 8-10 various small items
- wrapping paper, newspaper or brown paper
- felt pen
- scissors or exacto knife
- paper and pen for each guest
- optional prize: a chocolate bar or small treat for the winner

Once each detective has had a turn, let the birthday child open the box to reveal the contents. Detemine which detective was able to identify the most items and give a prize to the sharpest investigator.

> ★ "*Instead of having the kids wait for a long time for their turn, I let each guest have just a short time to identify only two of the items and then pass the box. It went around the table more quickly and everyone got several turns to solve the mystery.*" ★

■ Sleuth Slaying Mysteries

These mini-mysteries are great brainteasers and lots of fun too! The birthday child or host reads the mystery out loud to the guests. The guests are then asked to tell how they think the mystery is solved. Give them a few minutes; if the mystery is not solved, the answer is read aloud.

1. Alice wakes up one morning to find a pool of water beside her bed, some broken glass and Jill and Lisa lying dead on the floor. Alice knows she killed Jill and Lisa. How does she know?
   Answer: Jill and Lisa are guppies, and while Alice was asleep she knocked the fish bowl off her night table onto the floor.

2. A woman is found dead in bed with a sharp knife near her. There are no cuts on her body. What happened?
   Answer: The woman was sleeping on a waterbed. The knife she used to cut her apple the night before was beside her. It punctured the bed and she drowned in her sleep.

3. Three men enter a sauna, wrapped in towels, and one man is carrying a magazine. Two men leave and one man is found lying dead with a hole in his heart. There is a bit of water on the sauna floor. What happened?
   Answer: The man with the magazine stabbed the other man with an icicle.

■ Play 'Murder'

Murder is a game ideally played in a room where the door can be closed and one that is quite dark when the lights are turned off. You will need a regular deck of cards and to play, count out the exact number of cards as there are players and call it the 'playing deck'. Two specific cards must be included in the count; the ace of hearts and the two of clubs. Shuffle the cards and have each person draw one card from the playing deck. All players secretly look at their card and do not tell anyone which card they have. The leader will then explain that the person holding the ace of hearts is the 'detective,' and the person holding the two of clubs is the 'murderer'. No one else must know the murderer's identity. Now, the leader will ask the players to give the cards back and he explains the rest of the game step-by-step, using a demonstration to help the detectives understand.

- The 'detective' turns off the lights, making the room dark, and he leaves.

> **You'll need:**
> a deck of cards

- Everyone else moves around the room, including the murderer. While players are moving around, the murderer chooses a victim, whom he gently grabs by the arm.
- The person who is grabbed must scream and fall to the floor.
- As soon as the detective hears the scream, he knows that he must immediately return to the scene of the crime. He turns on the lights, and that signals everybody in the room to 'freeze' or to stop where they are and not move.

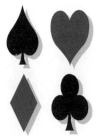

- The detective tries to solve the murder by asking questions. He can question anybody at the scene. *'Are you the murderer?'* Everyone must answer truthfully except the murderer, but the murderer *must* lie. The detective will eventually figure out who the murderer is by asking obvious questions like, 'Are you wearing shoes?' or 'What colour are your eyes?'
- If a player tells the truth, the detective knows that person is not the murderer. When the detective catches a player lying, he automatically knows that player is the murderer. The mystery is solved and the game is over.

Do you have red socks?

This game can be played again and again, as long as the guests are keen.

What's your name?

Food and Beverage Ideas

When it's time to feed the budding young detectives, here are two ideas they'll find worth investigating.

■ 'Mystery Drinks'

Sharpen the detectives' taste buds by trying these 'mystery drinks'. Mix together a variety of beverages and have the detectives try to figure out what ingredients are in their mystery drink.

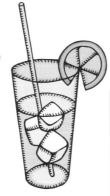

Examples:
- ginger ale with orange juice
- cranberry juice and orange pop
- milk and root beer
- 7-up and Coke

For an added challenge, blindfold the detectives before they try to guess the ingredients in their mystery drinks.

■ Magnifying Glass Cake

Assemble a magnifying glass cake to complement the detective theme.
- bake two round cakes
- stack the two cakes, with jelly in between for stability
- make the handle by positioning three jelly rolls firmly against the stacked cakes
- frost the cake in grey icing with a black outline around the magnifying glass portion
- on the top write: *Happy Birthday, Detective* _____

★ *"This theme cake was really easy to make and looked pretty impressive."* ★

Gift Opening Activity

Have fun with the gift opening by giving guests a few minutes to hide the presents that they brought to the party. Tell your guests, *'Your final mission for today is to hide the birthday gifts.'* Then, individually have each child take a turn to guide the birthday child to their gift by sayingg the word 'warmer' as they move closer to the gift, or 'cooler' if they move farther away from the gift. Remember to use names from the mystery identity game, for example, *'It's time for the birthday boy to find Sherlock Holmes' gift.'* or *'Okay, now where is Watson's?'*

> **Photo Opportunity**
> *The gift opening is a great time to take a photo of your birthday child individually with each guest.*

Thank You Cards

Give each guest a thank-you card with a message that's written backwards. It can be decoded with the mirror included in their 'top-secret' envelope (or loot bag).

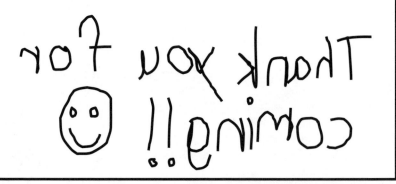

Attention all Detectives:
To decode this secret message – hold paper up in front of a mirror.

> ★ *"My son's friends still talk about our detective party and it was four years ago. They really liked how we kept referring to them as real detectives, 'Okay for our final mission, we must hide the presents—Scooby Doo can you begin?' A highlight was the mystery drinks, they kept tasting and tasting to try and figure out the exact ingredients. It was a great theme party."* ★

Handmade Cards for Mother's Day

Stamping is a great activity to do with the kids. Using some very simple techniques, you can make any card extra special. Follow the steps to creating homemade cards this Mother's Day, or any other important time of the year, to give to Grandmas, Aunties, Uncles, and friends. Keep it simple by using supplies you already have on hand, or you can borrow a few extra stamps, stencils or decorative scissors from friends.

Preparation

To prepare for stamping, cover your table with newspaper and arrange the supplies in the centre. Have the card stock measured, cut, and even folded ahead of time.

Basic supplies:
- cardstock or firm paper, in white or cream colour
- a variety of coloured paper, including cardstock or construction paper
- several stamps, rubber or foamy
- fine and wide-tipped markers in a variety of colours
- black stamp pad – be sure it is 'dye-based', so it won't bleed when you colour the image with markers
- glue stick
- blotter pad – inexpensive newsprint scrapbook or other scrap paper to test colours
- scissors

Optional supplies:
- finger painting paper (felt markers blend well on this 'glossy' paper)
- stencils
- make-up sponges (little sponge wedges found in the makeup section of drug stores)
- decorative-edged scissors
- sticky tack
- double-sided tape
- glitter glue
- paper cutter

★ *"We tried stamping cards a few different times and the image turned out horrible. It turned us off to stamping for a long time. The kids would get a little stamping kit as a gift and we'd simply put it aside. One day I saw my crafty friend stamping a card and the image came out perfectly; I asked her what the secret was. She said, 'Oh, you just have to be careful to press and hold the stamp for a few seconds.' I tried it and couldn't believe the difference. I was anxious to show the kids."* ★

Create a Double-Matted Card

1. **Choose a rubber stamp.** Select a stamp that you'd like to use on a card. Dab the stamp onto a stamp pad and press it on a piece of cardstock paper. Be sure to press the stamp and hold it down for a few seconds. Let the ink dry thoroughly.
2. **Colour the image.** Use fine-tipped felt markers to colour in the image, just like you would in a colouring book. Let the colouring dry completely.
3. **Trim the stamped paper into a square or rectangular shape.** Make sure your stamped image is centred on the paper.
4. **Cut out a piece of coloured mat paper.** Make this paper slightly larger than the size of the stamped cardstock.
5. **Glue the stamped image onto the mat paper.**
6. **Make the card.** Fold a new piece of cardstock into the shape of a card. You may need to trim the unfolded edges of the cardstock to achieve the desired card size for your matted image.
7. **Glue the matted image onto the front of the card.**
8. **Finish the card with a personalized message.** You now have a lovely home-made card.

Techniques to Enhance Your Card

Once you have the basic steps in mind, here are some ideas, tips and techniques that will expand your card-making repertoire.

■ Vary the Colour of Your Stamped Image

Vary the colour of your stamped image by using a coloured stamp pad. Or if the stamp you are using is mostly solid, you can use your wide-tip felt markers to apply colour directly onto the rubber stamp. Then *press and hold* the stamp down on the cardstock to transfer your image onto the paper.

■ Create a Background Effect Using a 'Masking Technique'

Example: Make a card with a snowman in the foreground and trees in the background. Stamp the snowman image on the card. Then, stamp the snowman image on a scrap piece of paper and cut it out, very close to the outline. Be careful not to cut *inside* the lines of the snowman. Apply a small blob of sticky tack to the back of the scrap snowman and place it over the 'good' snowman to *mask* it. Now, stamp the trees where you would like them on the card. Be especially careful to stamp right over top of the masked snowman because it will emphasize the background/foreground effect. Remove the scrap paper snowman and you have a lovely background effect, where the trees appear to be behind the snowman.

★ *"This is a great 3-D effect."* ★

■ Use a Variety of Stencils

- You can use any kind of stencil in card making; even real leaves or common shapes can be used as stencils to make interesting designs. Trace the shape with the guidance of the stencil and then colour it in.
- A more subtle design can be created by using stencils and a 'sponging technique'. Hold a wide-tip marker against a makeup sponge until the sponge absorbs some of the marker colour. Position the stencil on your paper and dab the makeup sponge around the edges of the stencil to produce a faint outline of the image. This makes a very soft, hazy look. Move the stencil and dab again, even overlapping the images. Soak up a second colour onto another makeup sponge and dab some more.
- In addition to the stencils that you outline, you can also use a 'negative' stencil where the shape has been cut out of the stencil. Sponge around the inside of the stencil to make a faint image of the shape itself.

■ Create an Interesting Background

Instead of using plain coloured paper as a background for your card, try creating a more interesting background paper, using a 'watercolour bathing technique'.

1. Use rubber or foam stamps that have solid images. Apply ink from a coloured stamp pad, or colour directly onto the stamp with a wide-tip marker. Press and hold the stamp onto the paper, then lift and twist the stamp and press down again.
2. Overlap images to fill in the whole page, leaving only a little white space. You can use a few different colours too, which adds variety to the background.
3. Next, dip a wide paintbrush (a fan-tip brush is perfect), into water and stroke from edge to edge of the paper. Repeat the dipping and stroking procedure until the paper is quite damp. Notice how the images start to bleed and the colour spreads beyond the stamped image.
4. Let the paper dry thoroughly. The result is several *blurred* images with shades of colour covering the paper.
5. Cut into pieces of background paper to use on your hand-made card.

> ★ *"We used the watercolour bathing technique to make beautifully coloured bookmarks to give for Valentines last year. Once the paper was dry, we cut them into pieces that were about 2" x 5 1/2". We put each classmate's name neatly across the front of the bookmark and our Valentine's message on the back. We received rave reviews!"* ★

■ Adding Details

Once the stamping and assembly of the card is complete:

- Use glitter glue to add some sparkle and shine to your card. Simply place a dab of glitter on an area to emphasize a specific detail, such as on the bands of colour on a rainbow.
- Use little embellishments or trimmings on a card to really make a particular detail stand out, such as a piece of ribbon, cord, string, raffia or a bow, miniature flowers, confetti, small pom-poms for noses, or even googly eyes.

   Example: If you have stamped a cupid, add a red pom-pom over his heart.

> *Having trouble with your glitter glue? If you seem to get more glue out of the tube than you wish, just blot it with paper towel to leave less behind on the paper. This creates a more subtle glitter effect rather than a big blob of glue, which takes forever to dry.*

■ Interesting Printing

Here are a few easy techniques to add a little flair to the printing on your card:

- ● Dots – write the words, then add a dot to each joint of the letter

- ★ Stars – draw a star at each joint

- ➢ Arrows – draw an arrow at each joint

- ♥ Hearts – draw a heart at each joint, or draw a heart to dot an 'i', or to make a period or comma

Stamping Troubleshooting

There are two common problems in rubber-stamping that can be discouraging to a beginner. The following troubleshooting tips will deal with those problems and make your cards seem more polished and sophisticated.

■ Only a partial image of the stamp comes out on the paper.

A common error made by beginners is to press the stamp onto the ink pad and then press *briefly* onto the paper. When the stamp is lifted there is very little ink transferred onto the paper, leaving only a partial image and a disappointed artist. The best method to 'ink the stamp' is to gently press the stamp onto the stamp pad, trying to apply the ink

Raising Kids…for the fun of it!

evenly, without overdoing it. When you place the stamp onto the paper use both hands to apply even pressure, PRESS AND HOLD the stamp down for a few seconds to allow time for the ink to transfer onto the paper. Do not 'rock' the stamp, as this will create a blurred image.

> **Tip:** Always do a 'test' image on a blotter pad or scrap paper first, before trying it on your good paper.

■ The image gets 'lost' when you colour it.

If your image seems to lose its detail when you colour it, you are using felt markers that are too dark. Unfortunately, even a large set of felt markers contain only a few light colours. If these few choices do not appeal to you, use a watercolour 'painting' technique to expand your colour selection. Using a tinfoil pie plate or dinner plate, you can create lighter colours. Scribble a patch of colour from your marker directly onto the pie plate. Dip a fine-tip paintbrush into water and touch it to the marker's colour on the pie plate. This will create a small patch of 'paint' (watered-down felt marker ink) which you can use to paint the areas of your stamped image. This technique works particularly well on watercolour paper or on glossy paper commonly used for finger painting.

> ★ *"My kids started making cards for Grandma and their friends when they were very young. Over the years we have picked up several rubber stamps and learned some new techniques. It has made our card-making fun and we're pretty proud of the cards we give away."* ★

Want to keep a special card made by your child?
- use it to label a box of decorations; for example, a Valentine's card for Valentine's decorations
- create a collage of their cards in a scrap book
- put the card in a frame
- slide the card into a photo album pocket

Family Fun

June 'De-Stressors'

Try out one or two of these activities with your kids to help relieve some stress through June and just to have a good laugh.

- have a watermelon seed-spitting contest
- indulge in a pudding or ice-cream eating contest—no hands allowed
- suck Jello through a straw
- go for an evening ice-cream trip in your pajamas

★ *"I'll never forget the look on my kids' faces the night I told them to hop in the van after they had put their jammies on. With some hesitation, they went outside and climbed in, still not knowing where we were going. As we pulled up to our favourite ice-cream shop, the biggest decision was whether we should go right inside or to just use the 'drive-through'. Eventually we opted for the latter. Almost every time we go for an ice-cream trip to that location, we remember our PJ night."* ★

Organized Living

Gifts Galore!

June is a busy time for gift giving. Ease the pressure by looking through these two great gift lists. Find a unique gift for Dad on Father's Day or the 'perfect' gift for that extra-special teacher.

Father's Day Gift Ideas

Activities
- make Dad his favourite dinner
- pre-arrange a golf game for Dad and a friend
- book a weekend for Dad and the kids to go fishing or camping

Gift Ideas
- framed artwork from the kids
- gift certificate for a back massage
- magazine subscription, such as Golf, Woodworking or Fortune 500
- something for the kids to assemble with Dad, like a bird feeder, patio bench or garden fountain
- mouse pad for the office, personalized with a photo of the kids
- accessories for his desk, e.g. business card holder, notepaper, pen or pencil container decorated by the kids
- accessories for his vehicle, e.g. a holder for his coins or sunglasses, a small tool kit, glove box emergency kit or collapsible shovel

- portable fire pit or hammock for the backyard
- special coffee or travel mug
- collage of the kids on a homemade calendar marked with important birthdays and complete with photos
- white cotton t-shirt decorated by the kids using fabric markers
- a classic movie on DVD
- a book by Dad's favourite author or a book featuring a biography of a professional athlete, a joke book, a home handyman book or a grilling cookbook
- sports equipment, like a tennis racquet, new ball glove, hockey stick or golf balls
- booklet of golf or movie passes
- wooden chess board set, backgammon or checkers

The 'Perfect' Teacher Gift

It's that time of the year when you'd like to show appreciation for your child's teacher. But choosing the right gift can often be quite a challenge, so here are some gift suggestions.

■ Gifts From Your Child

Consumable Gifts
- chocolates
- fruit basket
- bottle of wine
- specialty coffee or tea
- homemade fare – baking, chocolate almond bark, poppycock, nuts & bolts, jams, vinaigrettes, or salsa
- movie passes
- candles
- bath salts or beads
- note paper or writing paper
- small bouquet of fresh flowers from your own garden
- take them out for lunch or invite them over for a lunch at your home

> ★ *"One of the strategies I use when choosing teachers gifts is to find out how long they have been teaching. If the teacher is relatively new, then a coffee mug may be much needed and enjoyed. However, if the teacher is fairly 'seasoned', they may not be overly excited about their tenth coffee mug. Often in this case, I find a consumable gift is the best bet."* ★

Lasting Gifts
- pen
- magnet for filing cabinet
- mug
- napkins or napkin rings
- earrings or a pin
- hand-painted flower pot
- gardening kit – gloves, small shovel and seeds
- perennial plant – pot and bulbs
- a homemade craft – to decorate their home or classroom
- gift certificate for a bookstore
- book of inspirational messages or quotes
- journal
- magazine subscription
- photo of the teacher, either alone or with a group of kids

> **Do you have a green thumb?**
> *Share a favourite perennial with your child's teacher. Dig a root, put it in a pot or an ice-cream pail, and stick a bow on it. Include a short instruction card identifying the name of the plant, where it will grow best and its basic care.*

Raising Kids…for the fun of it!

★ *"One of my favourite gifts that we gave to a teacher was a photo of him. It was taken during a science class while he was 'in action', wearing a lab coat. I was able to get a picture where his expression was quite animated. We entitled it 'The Mad Scientist' and then framed it. My son signed and dated the back of the frame. From the stories that I heard, our gift received a lot of attention and was one of the biggest laughs on the last day of school."* ★

■ Class Group Gift Ideas

Have either the whole class or a small group of parents combine their budget for a large gift. This will provide more gift possibilities and variety for the teacher.

- a full spa treatment such as a manicure, pedicure, facial, and a massage
- restaurant gift certificate for a special dinner with their whole family
- golf passes
- gift certificate for a music or bookstore
- large ceramic or wooden pot of annuals from a greenhouse

Design a 'Memory Book' from the students:
1. Make a front and back book cover out of cardstock paper, approximately 9" x 12", which is just larger than the letter-sized sheets each student will use.
2. Write a title on the front cover and mount either a class group picture or small individual photographs of each child. Be sure to record the year for future reference.
3. Have each child submit a 8 ½" x 11" page on which they have drawn a picture, written a special message to their teacher and then signed it.
4. Put the book together with a coil binding, or simply staple the kid's pages between the two covers.

Memories of Mrs. Jenning's Class

The best thing about Mrs. Jenning's grade 2 class was:

The way she was always kind and made funny jokes.
From Tim

School's Out – Let's Celebrate!

Pack a picnic, order pizza, or go for dinner, but whatever you do —celebrate the end of the school year! Look through your child's report card together and talk about the year. Acknowledge the successes, discuss the challenges and look forward to the next school year. If you'd like to add a celebration gift, make it something they can use over the summer vacation. Ideas include a disposable camera, a snorkel set, a new beach towel, a stamp or coin collector's starter kit, a great big bouncy ball for summer games, 'mind bender' or puzzle books, a golf club or an art lesson.

★ *"When our kids were small, we'd celebrate the last day of school with a picnic at a playground. As they've gotten older, we usually let them choose a favourite restaurant to go to.. We all look forward to relaxing together, after a very hectic end of the year schedule. We'll often give them a special gift to acknowledge all their hard work. Usually it is something they can use through the summer like a great set of books or new sports equipment."* ★

Summer

Family Fun

Backyard Summer Fun

You don't have to go far to have some fun this summer—just head to the backyard and try out these great ideas.

Calling All Artists

■ Paint a Fence Mural

Purchase a large roll of paper from a craft store or go to your nearest newspaper office and request a newsprint roll end. You will need at least 10 feet (3 m) of paper that is about 3 feet (1 m) wide. Use strong adhesive tape to attach the paper to your fence. Mix up several colours of thick tempura paint, so it will not run down the paper. Use a variety of brushes to paint a scene across your back fence. Encourage your kids to let their imagination run wild or pick a theme, like *Farmyard Fun, Animals Galore, Super Summertime,* a playground scene, or try out an abstract design.

> ★ *"One summer vacation we called our 'Mural Summer'. I put up a big paper on the fence for my kids to paint on and they had a blast. In no time more children joined us from next door to help with the design. Everyone had so much fun; as soon as they were finished they wanted another sheet of paper. On the second mural, even more kids joined us from the neighbourhood and what a grand creation it was! The artistic energy was contagious. You'll never guess what we did for a birthday party activity that summer? ...You got it— we spread a large sheet of paper on the patio and put out a pile of felt pens and had everyone create a 'birthday mural'. It was a big hit."* ★

■ Rock Painting

Purchase several colours of 'patio paints' or acrylic paints and gather your small paint brushes. Search for smooth rocks to paint. Design a family of ladybugs or turtles, paint rock flowers or a sky scene with clouds and a sun. Place the decorated rocks in your flower bed or in a fancy dish on your patio table.

■ Sidewalk Chalk

Bring out a pail of sidewalk chalk and get your kids to make the longest hopscotch in the neighbourhood. Or, pick a theme and just go for it! Draw a big beach scene or a giant flower garden. What about creating a day at the zoo?

Design an Obstacle Course

Using any objects you have handy in your yard, garage or house, design an obstacle course in your backyard. Choose items that encourage different actions like rolling, climbing, jumping, hopping, slithering, squeezing through, or tip-toeing. Decide what order you would like to do the activities in, and then arrange the different items accordingly. Decide specifically what players will do at each station. For example, have the starting point in one corner of the yard. Begin with a basketball and bounce it five times, put the ball down on the ground and run to the next station. There is a lawn chair lying down and you must crawl through the legs, get up and go to next one and so on.

Examples:
- swing set in yard – swing once and jump off
- section of the lawn – to roll across to the next station
- a long 2" x 4" (5 cm x 10 cm) piece of wood – for tiptoeing across
- large cardboard box – slithering through
- hula hoop – for circling around hips five times
- small step ladder – for climbing and then jumping off
- lawn chair tipped on its side – for crawling through
- basketball – to dribble on the spot ten times
- a long rope – lay it flat and then hop with two feet together, back and forth over top in a zig-zag fashion
- funny hat, big shirt, and long socks – to put on in a designated spot, run to touch the fence, run back to the original spot, remove the clothing and leave them for the next competitor

Once the obstacle course is completely set up, let everyone try it out a few times so they know the order of the activities. Use a watch with a second hand or one with a stopwatch function. Time each participant as they go through the obstacle course and then arrange competitions. The competition can either be between family members or by having each player try to beat their own 'personal best' time. Invite the kids from the neighbourhood over and let them take a turn. After you've used one obstacle course for awhile, create another one to provide another challenge for the competitors. Designing the course is a big part of the fun!

★ *"One summer day the kids were getting a little bored. I was busy cleaning the garage. I found a long 2 x 4 in the shed, placed it on the grass and said, 'Okay, who can walk across this like we would on a balance beam?' They both tried and next we laid a lawn chair on its side in order to crawl through. At this point, we were right beside our swing set so I asked the kids what stunt they could do there. One of them replied, 'How about we swing one time and jump off, once we land we'll do a somersault.' The creativity had kicked in! The kids started gathering items from all over the yard and in the garage, ones they could use for some type of action. Our first obstacle course was under construction."* ★

Raising Kids...for the fun of it!

Have Some 'Science Fun'

■ Homemade Rockets

Place baking soda and vinegar in an empty film canister, put on the lid and shake well. Quickly place canister down on a hard surface like a sidewalk, with the lid facing up. Stand back to watch the 'rocket' launch!

■ Break the Surface Tension

Fill a small glass bowl with water and sprinkle a bunch of pepper on the surface of the water. Dip a toothpick into dishwashing liquid and dab it in the middle of the peppered water. The pepper quickly scatters away from the toothpick and to the sides of the dish. This is a great visual demonstration of *'breaking the surface tension'*.

■ Make a Liquid Tornado

Take a 2L clear, plastic pop bottle and fill it with water until it is about 1" (2.4 cm) from the rim. Add 3-4 drops of food colouring and 1 teaspoon (5 ml) of dish detergent. Screw the lid on tightly. Now put the bottle horizontally in front of you, away from your body. Holding it by both ends, shake it in a rapid, smooth, circular motion about ten times. Immediately turn the bottle upright. A tornado will emerge and twist around for several seconds— it's amazing! Once the water has settled down, you can repeat it again and again. Add glitter to the mixture in order to really see the 'swirling effect' of the particles.

> ★ *"I find the summer goes much more smoothly when I am armed with different activities for the kids to do. When they start to get bored and restless and often quite grumpy, I try to think of something fun. One time we tried some different science experiments. My son remembered one he learned in Scouts and then one from a science class. Our favourite one was watching the rockets launch."* ★

Silly Summer Fun

■ Pitch a Tent

Get out your tent, gather the sleeping bags and pillows, and go no further than your back yard. Tenting is a novelty anywhere and anytime—why not pitch one in your backyard this summer?

■ Lemonade for Sale

Set up a lemonade or iced-tea stand. You'll get a lot of business if you set up near the playground or at a sports field during a soccer or softball game. For something different, have all the proceeds go to a favourite charity.

■ Kids Pack the Picnic

Go for a picnic and let the kids do all the packing; food, drinks, blankets and activities. No parental assistance allowed—enjoy the surprises!

■ Gargling Contest

Have you ever gargled out your favourite song just for the fun of it? Get a group of kids together and try it outside, each using a mouthful of water. See who can identify the song you are gargling. How about trying your national anthem for Canada Day or the Fourth of July?

> ★ *"It's now tradition! We start every summer holiday with a tenting sleepover in our backyard. The kids start talking about it before school is even out."* ★

Raising Kids…for the fun of it!

Add a Little Drama

■ Make a Video

Give each child a videotape and let them take a turn with the video camera. They can create their own 'live' story—filming everything from friends, family, pets, their backyard, playground, to hobbies and other special interests.

■ Perform a Play

Choose a well-known fairytale, Disney story, or have the kids make one up of their own to perform. Include costumes, make-up, and pull out some props. Design a simple set and then let the kids enjoy a *theatrical day.*

■ Set up a Game Show

Suggest that the kids produce a TV game show or news broadcast.

★ *"One day I went outside to check on the kids and they were sitting in chairs lined up next to each other on our street. In front of them was a video camera propped up on a tripod. My son, Reid, had a microphone and was interviewing the others. I smiled to myself as I noted the kids ages; here was a group ranging from about five to twelve years old, all hanging out together and using their imagination. Now this was summer fun!"* ★

■ Play Charades

Charades is a game where players must act out a title without using any verbal clues. They can use hand signals and actions to help their team guess the answer.

Game Preparation
To begin the game, split kids into two teams. Give teams 10 minutes to write up charades that their opposition must act out. Choose titles from these four categories:

- book
- television show
- song
- movie

Make enough charades to give each person about three turns, for instance, a group of five players will need fifteen different charades. Once the charades are written, fold them closed and put them in a container. You'll need two containers, one for group A's charades, which group B has chosen, and another for group B's charades that group A created. Once all the charades are written up, have one member from team A come forward to act out or to give clues for the first charade.

To Keep Score
- Time each competitor and record how long it takes them to solve the charade. The maximum time limit is two minutes (which may be modified according to their ability).
- The team using the least amount of time to solve all of their charades is the winning team.

Solving the Charade
1. Identify the category:

Book – hold hands together in front of you and then open them as if you are opening a book in your hands.
Television Show – with your hands about chest height in front of you, make a rectangle shape to indicate a TV.
Song – lip-sync into an imaginary microphone while moving to an imaginary beat.

Movie – put one hand up near your chin, closed in a fist as if it is holding the bottom of a camera. The other hand rotates beside it pretending to crank the arm, as in an 'old movie camera'.

2. Follow these rules and techniques:
- No sounds or pointing at objects for clues.
- Use your fingers in the air to indicate how many words in the charade as well as which word you will act out first. Use fingers across your forearm to specify the number of syllables in a word, if necessary.
- If you need to identify what letter a word begins with, tap the side of your hand near your wrist, indicating '*starts with*', and tap once for 'a', twice for 'b', three times for 'c'

Raising Kids…for the fun of it!

and so on. To get to 'z' you do not want to tap 26 times, so the short cut is to begin tapping higher up on the arm, players will begin guessing the letter at 'm', two taps is 'n', three is 'o' and so on.

- If you want to use a rhyming word instead of the exact word in your charade, pull gently on your ear for *'sounds like'*. For example, if *force* is a word in your charade, you may choose to do *'sounds like' horse.* You can easily act out *horse* in comparison to a difficult word like f*orce.* Once your team has guessed *'horse'* from the actions you have done, point to the person who guessed horse and nod, then tap your wrist for a, b, c, and so on, up to 'f' for force.

- Use hand signals to stretch a word or to shorten it. For example, if you run on the spot and the group has guessed *run* but you want *running*. Put hands in front of you with fingers together and pretend to pull your hands away from one another in order to lengthen or 'stretch' *run* into *running*.

Charade example: The song 'Sunshine on my Shoulders'
- First hold an imaginary microphone as if you are singing. A player from your team responds with *'song'*; point to that person and nod your head.

- Next, hold four fingers in the air. Your team responds with *'four words'*; point and nod.

- If you choose to start with the first word to act out, put one finger in the air, your team shows their understanding by saying, *'first word'*. Point and nod again. Lay two fingers across your forearm to indicate two syllables as in 'sun – shine'; your team must respond with, *'two syllables'* and you nod.

- Now it is time to act out 'sunshine'. Possibly begin by acting out 'sun' and then lengthening it to 'sunshine'. If you are having trouble acting out 'sun', try *sounds like*, by pulling your ear. Once your team or a player has said, *'sounds like'* and you point and nod, hold up one finger. They'll probably guess, *'one'* and you nod, because *one* sounds like *sun*. Now you must tap up higher than your wrist, beginning at m, n, o, p, q, r, s. Point to the person that says, *'s'* and nod, they will understand that it 'sounds like' *one*, begins with s, and so the word is *'sun'*. Now lengthen it to 'sunshine', and begin acting out the next word. In this example, acting out the fourth word, which is 'shoulder', is quite easy, so do it next. Keep going until your team has guessed the entire title.

> ★ *"At one family gathering we decided to play charades. It took awhile to set up but it was really worth it. We laughed so hard as our 75 year old Nana got down on all fours and kicked her legs out, rearing her head up and down—she was a bucking bronc! Our youngest son laid down on his tummy with his arms and legs tucked in and slowly moved his head forward, we guessed 'turtle' right away. It was the fourth word in a movie so we instantly shouted out, 'Teenage Mutant Ninja Turtles'! We were right and he had acted out this difficult charade in about 20 seconds. Was he proud."* ★

Family Fun

Great Group Activities

Got a group of kids to entertain this summer? Whether it's just the neighbourhood kids, some overnight guests or a family reunion, try out some of these group games. There are games ranging from old-fashioned favourites like *Hide and Seek* and *Kick the Can*, to some new games that you can add to your summer repertoire.

Old Favourites

■ Hide and Seek

Play 'Hide and Seek' outdoors around the neighbourhood. Wait until dusk to make it even more fun.

Variation:
One person in the group hides. After the group

> ★ *"We had a riot playing the variation to Hide and Seek. The biggest challenge is keeping quiet as the hidden group gets larger and larger."* ★

counts to twenty, everyone goes to try and find the hidden person. The first one to find the hidden person joins that person in their hiding spot. The second one to find the *hiders,* who are now a pair, joins them too and so on, until the final person finds the whole hidden *group.* The last person to find the whole group is now 'it' and gets to hide first for the next round of the game.

■ Kick the Can

This game is best played at dusk when it is a challenge to see the players clearly. It is an exciting combination of hide and seek and tag. Decide amongst the group who is 'it' for the first round. That person stands near the can and closes their eyes as they count to 30, while everyone else hides. Once finished, the counter has to run around the neighbourhood and find everybody, while he also 'guards' the can.

The tricky part is that once a person is found, they must to get back to the can. The person who has just been found has to try to kick the can over before the counter tags them. If caught, they are the next person who is 'it'. If the hider kicks the can before being tagged, he is 'safe' and simply waits for the others. The person who is 'it' keeps trying to find the players that are still hidden and attempts to tag them before they each get back to the can to kick it. The play continues until someone is tagged before they kick the can and that particular player becomes 'it'. Therefore, they will be the 'counter' for the next round.

Raising Kids...for the fun of it!

Co-operative Games and Activities

Try some good co-operative fun, where there is no winner or loser but everyone is working *jointly* towards a common goal or combined score. These activities are especially good for multi-aged groups because you reduce the risk of the competition being uneven. This keeps it fun for everyone, rather than people competing against one another where some are older and potentially bigger, stronger or more skilled. In co-operative games everyone works together to compete against time or a better 'group' score.

■ Volleying Challenge

Arrange participants in a circle and see how many times you can consecutively bump, volley or hit the ball before it touches the ground. Use a balloon for very young children, a light weight beach ball for a bit older, and a volleyball for those in grade five or higher. Count each time someone hits the ball to keep it in the air, not allowing it to touch the ground:
'*one, two, three,* and so on...' until the ball hits the ground.
When you count out loud it motivates players to keep the ball in the air and they will try even harder. Each time it hits the ground, you begin counting at *one* again and together keep trying to beat your highest 'group' score.

■ Blanket Ball Fun

In a group of four or more, with each person holding a corner of the blanket, place a lightweight rubber ball in the centre. Next, try one of these three co-operative games:
- Try to move the ball clockwise around the outside of the blanket without the ball falling off. See how many rotations you can do in a row, before the ball hits the ground.
- As a group, throw the ball up into the air and then catch it again on the blanket. See how many times your group can successfully throw and catch the ball consecutively on the blanket before it hits the ground.
- If you have two groups of three or four and two blankets, toss the ball back and forth from one blanket to the next. Count out loud again and see how high the two groups can get together.

■ Kickball

Kickball is a game that's played like baseball except the ball is kicked instead of batted. Since kicking is an easier skill, a child of any age can play with success and therefore can have a lot of fun. All you'll need is a heavy rubber ball and four bases. Split into two teams; one goes in the field and the other is *up to bat*. The game begins with the pitcher rolling the ball to the first kicker, who is standing beside home plate. If the ball rolls over home plate, it is a 'strike'. The kicker has three chances or three strikes to achieve a successful kick or one that lands within the boundaries of the field.

Once the ball is kicked out into the field, there are three ways for the fielders to put a 'kicker' out:

> **No bases for the game?** *Use the floor mats from your car.*

1. Fly ball – if the ball is kicked high in the air and then caught by a fielder before it touches the ground, the kicker is out.
2. Forced out rule – if a fielder catches the ball and throws it to the first baseman before the runner gets to first base, the kicker is out.
3. Hitting the runner between the bases – if a fielder hits the runner with the ball while they are running between bases, they are out. This is a rule unique to kickball, don't try it with a baseball!

When there are three 'outs', kickers must go out to the field and fielders come in to take their turn at kicking. The game is finished when each team has had an equal number of turns kicking and fielding and when everyone is ready to call it a game!

> ★ *"We love playing kickball. It's a great game because it is easy and fun to play but one of the best parts is that it is multi-aged. Even Grandma will come out and play with us, she is still able to kick the ball and run carefully around the bases."* ★

Raising Kids…for the fun of it!

Family Fun

Family Golf – Play 'Best Ball'

Try this golf game variation with your family while the kids are young and learning to golf. Your 'family goal' is to get the lowest collective score. It is easier to achieve a lower score in this game than in a regular game of golf because four people are working together on one score. In fact, there are four chances to make each shot whether it is a drive, fairway shot or a putt.

To start, everyone drives off the first tee box. Next, you determine who drove the furthest or whose ball is in the best position from which to take the second shot. Pick up the other three player's golf balls and carry them to that point. All golfers will now take their second shot from this location. Continue in this fashion until you reach the green. Once you are on the green, everyone takes a putt from the ball that has landed closest to the pin.

★ *"One of our favourite activities in the summer is 'Family Best Ball'. It's such a relief when you've duffed your drive, to simply pick up your ball from where it landed, walk up and drop it beside the longest drive. This year our youngest was able to 'help' drive the golf cart, our eleven year old sunk a ten foot putt and our son who is thirteen challenged his Mom and Dad with almost every shot he took. We had a great round and together we almost parred the course."* ★

Variations in pairs that add a little 'friendly' competition:

■ Two-Ball Best Ball
Split into two teams of two golfers. Play 'best ball' in pairs with the same guidelines as described above in family best ball. In this variation, the pairs compete against each other and try for the lowest score between them.

■ Alternate Shot
In this game, you split into teams and alternate shots on every hole so that person #1 drives the ball, person # 2 takes the next shot, then person #1, and so on, until ultimately your team sinks the putt. The object of the game is to be the pair that gets the lowest score.

If you have two families, make teams of Dads vs. Sons or Moms vs. Daughters, or even one family vs. another.

Teaching Money Management

There's a whole set of money management skills you want your children to learn before they leave home, such as budgeting, saving and making good financial choices. One way to effectively introduce and develop many of these skills is by implementing an allowance system.

> *"Well-educated parents demand that their children excel in the arts, in education, and sports, but think nothing of unleashing them into this complex world with little or no financial knowledge."*
>
> Inez Dyer, Edmonton Journal

An allowance will definitely give your children experience in managing their own money. One important factor is that you, as a parent, need to allow your children to make mistakes and live with the consequences. Making a poor financial decision with a small weekly allowance as a child is low risk, since there is not much money at stake. However, practising poor money mangement as an adult can be quite costly—there are whole paychecks to squander and consequences that are long lasting. Teach money management while your kids are young to prepare them for future financial decisions.

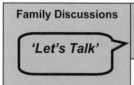

What does managing allowance teach?

- $ the value of money
- $ the value of possessions and the importance of taking good care of them
- $ how to delay gratification
- $ how to control impulse buying
- $ how to save
- $ how to share your resources by sponsoring a charity

Allowance is a topic many families struggle with. Parents ask themselves several questions, such as: *When do I start giving an allowance? How much do I give to each child? Do I tie allowance to chores around the house? Exactly how do I implement an allowance system?*

Summertime is a good time to 'tackle the allowance issue'. There are increased opportunities to spend money and usually more financial decisions for children to make. Children also have more time to do chores and earn money. Also, in summer, parents have more time to calculate and administer whichever allowance procedure they choose to implement.

How much allowance?

There are many factors to consider when determining the amount of allowance that is suitable for each child. First and foremost, the amount is dependent upon what you decide to make your children financially responsible for. Are they expected to pay for their clothes, their outings such as bowling or movie admission, video rentals, treats, gifts for the family or for their friends? This will vary considerably with your child's age; a preschooler may be responsible for only a few things such as special treats or little outings, therefore a dollar per week may be sufficient. With a 7-10 year old child, you may want to add more responsibility. In addition to paying for activities, perhaps you'll add family gifts to their budget. As children get into the 11-13 age bracket, you might decide they'll be in charge of gifts for friends and perhaps their own clothing. Increasing financial responsibility as they get older is a good method to follow. Ultimately, by the time they are eighteen and getting ready to be out on their own, they will be more prepared to budget and spend money wisely.

> *Set clear expectations of what their allowance money needs to cover and then your child can decide how to save or spend the remainder of their money.*

Another allowance factor to consider is the amount of chores your children do. An older child is capable of contributing more to running the family household and therefore should be given a larger allowance. A raise in allowance can natually accompany an increase in age—but be certain there is a congruent increase in contribution or household reponsibilities.

A very important consideration when deciding how much money to pay for allowance is to ensure your child has *enough* resources to teach money management. A mere $2-3 per week will only give them enough for spending money and could ultimately teach them to spend everything they earn. Using a basic guideline of $1.00 per week per year of the child's age will be enough money to actually teach him/her money management. For example, an eight year old would be given $8.00 per week or $32 per month. This will give them *enough* money to make financial decisions about spending money, savings, gifts, charity and so on.

How often to pay allowance?

Establish a regular time to give allowance. It is something kids will count on and it will build trust and dependability between the two of you. Once a month is easy to remember and will give children a greater lump sum of money to manage. However, for younger children, it may be too long to wait or too much money to handle, so a weekly pay schedule may be more suitable for them.

A good tip for keeping track of 'allowance paid' is to put the details on your calendar. Write when it was paid and the amount that was given. You can also record if any money was loaned out ahead of payday.

Is allowance tied to chores?

Do I automatically pay out allowance every week or should it be determined by my kid's chore load? You will read conflicting ideas from the experts on this issue. Some experts think a child needs a consistent income in order to learn money management and therefore they promote regular allowance dispersements. In this theory, children do chores because they are contributing to the household and not because they receive payment. Just as parents are not paid for cooking or cleaning, neither are their kids.

However, a completely opposite theory is to teach children the 'no work – no pay' lesson early in life because ultimately that is how the *real world* operates. In other words, if they do not complete their chores in a week, they will simply not be paid. This particular method of paying allowance is much harder to implement; children will have to keep a checklist that parents will need to monitor. This is an on-going, time-consuming task. A major benefit of this philosophy is 'chore-motivated children'. They will want to contribute more and increase their chore load simply because they will be paid more. Unfortunately a possible reaction could be a child saying, 'I have enough money already, you can do the dishes yourself!'

★ *"When our family implemented the 'no work, no pay' theory, I was so impressed! The kids were coming to me and asking, 'What needs to be done?' 'Can I unload the dishwasher today?' 'Mom, do you need the car washed?' It was everything I had hoped for. However, when our six year old asked, 'Can I have some money, I just made my bed?'—I realized that any allowance system has its pros and cons."* ★

Raising Kids…for the fun of it!

Making Good Choices

■ Good Value

It is important to talk about the *value* of a purchase with your child. Once you've discussed an item, allow your child to make the decision. If they go ahead with the purchase and it is a poor choice, they must live with the consequences. The experience will hopefully help them make a better choice next time. Discuss the long-term value of a purchase. For example, what if your child has outgrown his skates and needs new ones, but it is already the month of January? Guide him to consider the *timing* of his purchase. In this case, he only has a couple of months left in his hockey season because it wraps up at the end of March. He will not use the skates again until August or September which is almost half a year. If he is at a stage where he is still growing quickly, there is a chance that the skates will not fit in the fall. Is it a good time to purchase new skates or are used ones his best value for the remainder of this hockey season? If you take the time now to help your child look at the pros and cons of a specific purchase, they'll learn to do so for themselves in the future.

> *The dollar store is a great place for young children to compare value, since the prices are all the same.*

■ 'Wants' vs. 'Needs'

How do I teach the difference between 'wanting' or really 'needing' something? Once children are responsible for purchasing items of basic 'need', such as clothes, parents have an additional teaching opportunity. Begin by asking your child if they really *need* the item or if is simply a *want*. Purchases of either kind are definitely acceptable, but children must learn to consider their resources. Spending too much money on *wants* rather than focusing on *needs*, could lead to a shortage of money for items that they truly need when the time comes. Learning to distinguish between what you want and what you can afford is an important life skill.

> ★ *"Once our guidelines were established on what the kids were responsible for, most of our conversations about spending went smoothly. Whatever it was that they asked for, whether it was something they really wanted or actually thought they needed, I often responded with, 'Sure you can buy that ...with your own money.' It was easier for them to determine how important a purchase was when they had to spend their own hard-earned cash."* ★

How do we teach about savings?

There are many ways to encourage savings. Short-term savings are certainly the easiest. To get your child involved in the saving process, have them focus on something they want or need in the *immediate* future. Saving can be especially successful if the item is of special interest to them, such as a purchase for a favourite hobby or sport. Suppose your child is a ski enthusiast and it is early October with ski season just around the corner. She needs a new pair of ski boots and you tell her that she is expected to pay for half of the purchase price. She will probably be highly motivated to save for the boots because she needs them right away and she will probably be successful in her saving goal. This positive experience will likely have a ripple effect for future short-term saving.

Long-term saving is a more difficult concept to teach. One long-term strategy is to actually make saving compulsory. For instance, if their allowance is $8 per week, have your child put $1 in their saving jar right off the top. If you instill the habit of saving at an early age, it will be a natural part of their money management routine and they will have acquired an invaluable life skill. Furthermore, a dollar saved per week at a young age has a substantial compounded value, and as a parent you have fostered a great little 'investor', as well as a saver!

What about charity?

Teach charity early. If children put their *own* money in the collection plate at church or take their *own* money to school for a fundraiser, it gives them a sense of contribution. This again, has long-term value. If we encourage the habit of *giving* early, it will be part of their natural routine. Children may need encouragement to start the process of giving. A good tip is to choose a charity that has had a direct impact on your child. For instance, they could give to the Heart Association if a grandparent has a heart condition. This is much more meaningful to your child than donating some of their resources just for the 'sake of giving'.

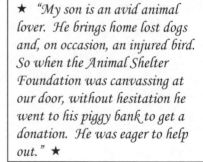

★ *"My son is an avid animal lover. He brings home lost dogs and, on occasion, an injured bird. So when the Animal Shelter Foundation was canvassing at our door, without hesitation he went to his piggy bank to get a donation. He was eager to help out."* ★

Raising Kids…for the fun of it!

Allowance Summary

Find an allowance system that works for *your* family. You'll want one that suits your philosophy, your family's needs and resources and the time you have available to implement it. Once you've decided how much to pay and how often, establish whether or not you want their allowance tied to chores around the house. Capitalize on all the teaching opportunities; use allowance scenarios to discuss good value, wants vs. needs, saving and charity. You will have to evaluate your system from time to time and assess whether or not it is teaching the money management skills that you believe are important.

Other Financial Suggestions

$ **Open a bank account for each child.** Choose a bank that provides a monthly statement as a record of deposits, withdrawals and the interest paid. Many banks have special accounts for kids that have no monthly fee. When your child is ready, allow them the responsibility of a banking card.

> ★ *"My daughter turned 13 and we gave her the privilege of having her own bank debit card. This meant easier access to her bank account and we discussed the risk of having cash on hand, virtually at anytime. In the beginning, she made a few impulse purchases that she regretted, but overall it didn't take her long to use the debit card more cautiously."* ★

$ **Talk about monthly expenses.** Discuss the cost of running a household with your children. Children do not have to know the specific details of your income nor do you have to burden them with financial worries, but discuss the monthly bills like heating, water and groceries. The more they learn now, the less surprises there will be in the future.

$ **Look at a monthly charge card statement together.** Discuss the amount of interest that would be charged this month if the amount owing was not paid in full.

$ **Have children help find strategies to reach a financial goal.** For example, your family wants to go on a special weekend trip at the end of the month. Brainstormon how everyone can help finance the trip. Some ideas might be giving up 'pizza night' for two Fridays or hand-washing the vehicles instead of taking them to the carwash. Everyone will feel a sense of contribution.

Tackling the 'To Do' List

Gather the kids together and ask them to help you compile a 'To Do' list of weekly jobs, maintenance items or bigger projects. Then try out one of these strategies to get everyone tackling the list throughout the summer.

Pick a 'Surprise Chore'

Write each task out on a separate piece of paper, fold and place in a container labelled 'Summer Job Jar'. When it's time to work, pull out a surprise chore from the job jar.

Examples of Weekly Jobs
- mow the lawn
- dust living room
- clean bathroom
- tidy your bedroom

Keep a master list of the tasks and check them off as they are completed.

Bigger Projects or Maintenance Items
- clean and vacuum out a vehicle
- weed a section of the garden or a flower bed
- paint picnic table
- do some filing
- sort toys and clean out containers
- clean your desk
- de-clutter one area of your room
- go through your school stuff and decide what to keep in a scrapbook
- clean your closet, sort through and remove clothes that are not being worn

★ *"We used a 'Job Jar' one summer to have a little fun with our chores. The kids could either choose a task from the jar or one from the master list. They both began by choosing a job from the jar, but then it was funny to see how their personality traits came through. My son soon found that he preferred to make a choice from the list and be guaranteed a job that he didn't mind doing—he wanted to be in control. My daughter, however, liked to take the chance and she often chose from the job jar instead."* ★

Raising Kids…for the fun of it!

Give me 'One Hour per Day'

Another way to involve the kids in summer chores is by using the 'one hour per day' technique. Have each child commit to giving one hour each day to household or outdoor tasks. You'll be pleasantly surprised at how fast those odd little jobs around the house are completed.

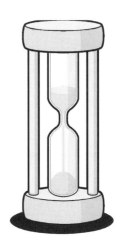

> ★ *"Jobs just disappeared off my list when we tried the 'one hour per day' system. Since there typically is a lot of free time in the summer, it seemed reasonable to ask for just an hour a day. They 'bought in' to the idea fairly fast. As a result of daily work being done by everyone, a huge weight was lifted off my shoulders. I had more time for summer fun and the boys all felt pretty proud of what they'd accomplished too. As with many ideas, this work schedule didn't last forever, but it sure worked for awhile in our home."* ★

Work like a 'Team'

Introduce the 'team' concept—explain that all members of your family are like members of a *team*. You are never too old or too young to be part of the 'family team'. You can work together to keep the house tidy, put a meal on the table or organize the basement. Not only will the job get accomplished quicker but also all members of the family will feel a sense of contribution.

One example at mealtime:
- Mom – preparing the main course
- Dad – making a salad
- One child – setting the table and helping to put the food on the table
- Another child – unloading the dishwasher, if needed

The meal is put on the table in a jiffy and everyone has helped.

> ★ *"Nothing feels better than when our whole family is working together to accomplish a specific job. It feels like we are a 'unit'. It's great when we can count on everyone to help out."* ★

> *Try a ten minute pick-up by everyone just before bedtime. It saves one person having to do it all by themselves.*

Kids 'n Cooking

Has your child ever prepared a meal for the entire family? Summer is a good time to teach them. Be patient, it will take some time for your child to learn their way around the kitchen. Start out simply so you can make the process enjoyable while you build this life-long skill.

> ★ *"The look of pride on my son's face after he made his first meal for the family, made me wish I had encouraged him to cook sooner!"* ★

■ Breakfast Possibilities

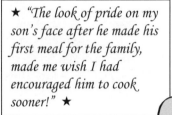

- pancakes from a mix, served with back bacon and sliced oranges
- scrambled eggs with toast and fresh fruit
- grilled sausages with toasted bagels and cream cheese

■ Lunch Ideas

- macaroni and cheese, veggies and dip, with sliced bananas mixed into yogurt for dessert
- grilled ham and cheese sandwich with carrot sticks, fruit and dip for dessert
- soup with cheese and crackers, with sliced apples

■ Supper Suggestions

- hot dogs, peas, french fries, with ice cream for dessert
- tacos with lettuce, tomato, cheese, sour cream, salsa and guacamole
- homemade pizza
- baked chicken breasts and potatoes with a salad made from a kit

It's Travel Time!

Planning a road trip over the summer vacation? Whether you are going near or far, a little preparation can help get you there and save your sanity too. Here are a few ideas of what to do before you *'hit the road'* as well as several ideas to keep kids busy and entertained during the trip. These tips can take you a looooong way.

Before the Road Trip

■ Get the Kids Packing

As children grow older, they can be involved in the packing. Discuss where you are going and what you will be doing, and ultimately what they

will need. Have them make a checklist of items to pack. If they use a computer, the list can be modified and used over and over again. It will not only teach them some responsibility, but also save you a lot of time.

Give each child a knapsack to hold items that will entertain them on the trip. Individual knapsacks:
- *hold everything in one place*
- *fit nicely into the car*
- *can be easily transported to be used in a restaurant, hotel or at a campsite*

★ *"We gave our kids the responsibility to pack for themselves. One time my son left his swimming trunks at home and rather than run to a store to pick up a new pair for him, he had to wear his athletic shorts for swimming that week. It was a bit uncomfortable, so the next time we went away you can bet he remembered to pack his trunks."* ★

■ Plan for Fun and Healthy Snacks

Choose smart snacks. Limit the amount of sugar intake as it can make some children hyper or *antsy* which is not a good thing when travelling and being confined to the car for lengthy periods. Instead, choose snacks that are savoury, like cheese and crackers, veggies, cheese sticks, yogurt tubes, fruit, nuts or trail mix.

Fun with twisted pretzels. Pretzels are a great snack and can also be used for a bit of fun. See what letter you can make out of each pretzel as you bite pieces off? *I've got a 'C'. Look at my 'X'.* Try a game where you have to identify a person's name that starts with the letter you created, such as D for Diane.

Build edible necklaces or bracelets. Fill individual zippered, plastic bags with Cheerios and a piece of shoestring licorice for each child. They will be able to thread their own necklace or bracelet. Add a few Fruitos for colour and pizzazz.

Jellybean taste tests. Bring along gourmet jellybeans and have a 'taste test'. One person chooses a jellybean colour to hand out; they'll require as many jelly beans of one colour as there are participants. Each person must close their eyes as they are handed the jellybean (except the driver ☺), so they cannot see the colour, which could be a clue to the flavour. Once they've put the jellybean into their mouth, they can open their eyes as they slowly chew it and try to determine the flavour. Give every person a turn to choose which jellybeans they'll distribute for the others to guess the flavour.

Homemade trail mix. Prepare individual bags filled with homemade trail mix. Choose ingredients specific to each person's preferences and/or allergy restrictions. Here are some possibilities:

- raisins or Craisins
- milk chocolate chips
- dried fruit, e.g. banana chips
- peanuts
- cashews

- yogurt covered raisins
- almonds
- m & m's
- sunflower seeds
- pumpkins seeds

■ Plan for Travel Fun

Plan for frequent stops. When travelling with children, allow extra time for frequent stops. Bring along a skipping rope or an inflatable beach ball to play with during the breaks.

Pack a picnic lunch. Instead of trying to have your kids sit quietly in a restaurant, pack a picnic lunch. Stop at a park or a playground to eat and let them burn off some excess energy afterwards.

> Bring along a cooler stocked with ice, drinks, fruit and sandwiches for the crew. Add a water bottle for everyone and possibly a damp cloth in a plastic zippered bag for easy clean up.

Purchase or copy extra maps for the children. Your kids can follow the driving route on their map by using a highlighter marker from one location to the next. Map reading is a great skill to develop. Have fun estimating the time it will take to get to the next main center or to the final destination.

> ★ *"I find planning ahead for entertainment in the car or plane, is as important as making reservations or other travel details. If my kids have a variety of activities at their fingertips, our trip starts off well and is more enjoyable for everyone."* ★

Raising Kids...for the fun of it!

Pack a 'surprise bag'. Include toys the kids haven't played with for awhile and also put in a few new items that you've purchased. Wrap up some of the toys or small gifts. When the trip is becoming unbearable, have each child pick an item from your *magic bag of goodies*. Something 'new' could entertain them, maybe even for hours.

Small, inexpensive gifts from the dollar store that you could wrap individually:
- mini deck of cards
- book light or mini flashlight
- book of riddles
- crossword puzzles
- small hand-held mini games

★ *"My friend drove from Toronto to Edmonton for a family visit one summer. I thought she was crazy and asked how they all made it in one piece. She shared a few of her 'secrets' and one was how she wrapped up some surprise gifts and passed them out as needed through the trip. Her gifts were not very substantial or expensive, but the kids were still excited about them. I could tell because as they arrived at our home, the first thing they wanted to do was show off their new little toys and the neat novelty pencils."* ★

Take a trip to the library. Look for a variety of books on tape or CD. Borrow ones suitable for different members of your family. If you aren't using individual headphones, find selections that will work for everyone. Be sure to get input from the kids on the audio books.

■ Organizational Tips

Use a small plastic tote box for storage. The tote will hold several items for travel, and the lid can double as a writing surface or a larger surface to play cards on.

Tie a pencil to a clipboard. Your child will have a smooth firm surface to write on, and the pencil never gets lost. Use a mechanical pencil that does not require a pencil sharpener.

Purchase a car organizer. They are ideal for keeping everything in one place. Hang it near the kids so they'll have it within their reach. Ensure that your organizer has many different compartments and it will be a novelty for your child to go through them to see what's inside. Stock it with a variety of snacks, toys and activities.

Mesh drawer liners can cover a piece of cardboard or a tray to create a non-slip surface for playing cards or dice.

During the Trip

■ Avoid Travel Sickness

Before you hit the road, a factor to consider is how well your children travel physically. Are they prone to motion sickness? Do they need to choose their activities according to the state of their stomachs? Planning ahead in this regard can really affect the overall success of the travelling portion of your vacation. If your child is prone to car sickness, try these tips:

- **Have children keep their eyes on the road for the first part of the trip.** They must be looking forward, rather than out the side of the vehicle, where they see the trees and other scenery going by very quickly. Otherwise, it may upset their equilibrium.

- **Keep a window open.** Fresh air circulating in the vehicle is often helpful to the child.

- **Keep children hydrated**. Encourage them to have small but regular sips of water.

- **Stop when necessary.** If a child becomes ill, get them out of the vehicle. Stopping the motion will ease the nausea. It may be essential, especially on a hot day, to have them lie down in the shade for awhile.

- **Try out motion sickness strips.** These strips attach to the bumper and are designed to cut down on the static electricity in the vehicle.

> **Travel Sickness Kit**
> - a small pail with a lid
> - roll of plastic bags that can be used as liners for the pail
> - wet wipes or a damp face cloth in a plastic zipper bag
> - extra water bottle
> - package of mints
> - change of clothes or at least a clean t-shirt to help the child freshen up

> ***Avoid the fast food trap:***
> *Greasy food can tend to make you feel sleepy and queasy since it doesn't digest easily. Opt for lighter fare instead such as sandwiches and fruit.*

Raising Kids…for the fun of it!

■ Car Games and Activities

Here are some games easily played in the confined space of a vehicle.

Alphabet Games

Going through the alphabet, name a place (town, city, country or even continent) beginning with the letter 'A'. The rule is that everyone must name a different place, so four people might guess Asia, Antarctica, Albuquerque, Africa. The next letter is 'B', Boston, Bermuda, Bosnia, Barbados, and so on.

> ★ *"We play the alphabet game almost every trip we take. It's a good game for all ages."* ★

Name the Animal

Pick a topic such as 'animals'. One person begins by naming a certain animal. The next person must then say an animal that begins with the letter that the first animal's name ended. Example: Lio<u>n</u> ends with 'n' so the next animal begins with 'n' such as new<u>t</u>. Newt ends in 't' so the next person must say an animal that begins with 't', like tiger. This particular game might go on with <u>r</u>hinocero<u>s</u>, <u>s</u>nak<u>e</u>, <u>e</u>lephan<u>t</u>, and so on.

Variation: You can play this same game using other topics, like cities or names of people. The teen's version could be names of bands, musicians, books or movies.

'Hum-A-Tune'

Each person takes a turn humming a tune and the rest of the participants try to guess the name of the song. Whoever guesses correctly gets to hum the next selection.

Possible tunes to hum:	Example:
• Songs from TV shows	*'The Adam's Family', 'Barney' or 'Caillou'*
• Christmas carols	*'Rudolph, the Red-nosed Reindeer'*
• Childhood favourites	*'Wheels on the Bus'*
• Church hymns	*'Jesus Loves Me'*
• Campfire songs	*'My Bonnie Lies Over the Ocean'*
• Lullabies	*'Lullaby and Goodnight…'*
• Other favourites	

Variation: If one person is not being successful in guessing and therefore not getting a turn to hum, go in a specific order to give everyone a chance. Try going clockwise or from youngest to oldest.

> ★ *"Hum-a-tune is a hilarious game! It is really hard to carry a tune while you hum and so we end up laughing ourselves silly."* ★

20 Questions

This game begins with one person choosing a word from one of the following categories: person, place, plant, animal or object. They must keep the word confidential and then the 20 questions begin. All questions must be able to be answered with either a 'yes' or a 'no'. For example, if the category is *animals*, you can ask if the animal lives in a zoo (yes/no) but you cannot ask where the animal lives.

To begin, guessers will want to identify which category the word belongs to, so start with a question like, *'Is it a person?'* The group will ask questions individually until someone gets the answer, or to a maximum of 20 questions, whichever comes first. If 20 questions are reached and the correct answer has not been guessed, the answer is given out loud. Another round begins with a different player choosing an item from one of the five categories and the questioning begins again.

Example 1:
1. Is it an object? (if 'no', proceed to the next category)
2. Is it a place? (no)
3. Is it a person? (if 'yes', guessers try to narrow it down)
4. Is it a female? (no)
5. Is it someone in our family? (no)
6. Is it someone at school? (no)
7. Is it someone who is over 20 years old? (yes)
8. Do I personally know them? (no)
9. Is it someone on TV? (yes)
10. Are they famous for acting? (no)
11. Are they known for their singing? (no)
12. Is he an athlete? (yes)
13. Is it Tiger Woods? (no)
14. Is he famous for hockey? (no)
15. For basketball? (yes)
16. Is it Michael Jordan? (yes!)

> The person who is answering keeps track of how many questions have been asked in total.

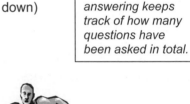

Example 2:
1. Is it a person? (no)
2. Is it an object? (yes)
3. Is it bigger than a breadbox? (no)
4. Is it found in a car? (no)
5. Is it found in a home? (yes)
6. Does the object perform an important function? (yes)
7. Is it electric? (yes)
8. Is it a hairdryer? (no)
9. Is it an iron? (no)
10. Is it found in the kitchen? (yes)
11. Is it a coffee maker? (no)
12. Is it a blender? (yes!)

Raising Kids…for the fun of it!

Vehicle Scavenger Hunt

Make a list of items to look for in your travels and check them off as you spot them. Each person can have a list of their own or everyone in the car can work together on one list.

- ❑ yellow car
- ❑ black truck
- ❑ dog in a vehicle
- ❑ green van
- ❑ 5 semi trucks
- ❑ cow
- ❑ horse
- ❑ deer
- ❑ overpass
- ❑ license plate from out of state/province
- ❑ punch buggy (Volkswagen)
- ❑ flag
- ❑ river
- ❑ red barn
- ❑ white fence
- ❑ hay bale
- ❑ communication tower
- ❑ other items that would be specific to the area you are travelling in, such as a boat or waterfall

Variation 1:
Count how many of one thing you see during a certain portion of your trip, for instance, how many flags can you count from Edmonton to Red Deer?

Variation 2:
Keep a running tally of the number of license plates you see from other provinces or states.

Variation 3:
Keep a tally of the type of vehicles that you pass or meet on the road.
- ❑ Fords
- ❑ Chevrolets
- ❑ Chryslers
- ❑ Semi-trailer trucks
- ❑ R.V.'s
- ❑ Others

> ★ *"The scavenger hunt kept the kids entertained a long time."* ★

Memory Game

The first person says, '*I packed my suitcase and in it I put* _____ '. Each consecutive person must recite all the previously packed items, plus add one of their own. For instance, player #1 says, *I packed my suitcase and in it I put my comic book.* The next person must say *comic book* and then something they packed for instance, *swimsuit.* The third person will have two items to remember and then add one of their own. Go through the group many times, if you have five people in the car, after two turns each, there will be 10 things to remember. See how high you can go and still remember all the items.

Variation: Players must go in alphabetical order, *I packed my suitcase and in it I put an **a**pple, **b**rush, **c**ool shades, **d**eodorant, etc.*

Make up Rhymes or Limericks

Here's a rhyming song to use with the younger crowd.

> Begin with: *Willabee, Wallabee Woo*
> *An elephant sat on you.*
>
> Now fill in the blanks:
> *Willabee, Wallabee Rustin*
> *An elephant sat on _____.*
> (Pause to give the group a chance to fill in the blank and then all say *'Justin'*)
> *Willabee, Wallabee Baron,*
> *An elephant sat on _____. (Sharon)*

Older children are able to make up limericks. Limericks are poems that have five lines, where the first, second, and fifth lines rhyme, as well as the third and fourth. Here are two examples:

> There was a young man from Peru,
> Who dreamt he was eating a shoe.
> He awoke with a start,
> He thought it not smart,
> That poor dear young man from Peru.

> There was a cute gal who was silly,
> Who traveled a road that was hilly.
> Her stomach got sore,
> And she cried out 'no more'
> The trip that she took was a dilly!

> ★ *"It took a little while to learn how to make up the limericks, but soon the kids got into it. They started making up silly words and being quite outrageous."* ★

Other Games and Activities

- **Magnetic or travel games** – chess, checkers, backgammon, Boggle, Yahtzee, 4 in a Row, Battleship, Sorry or Monopoly
- **Drawing pad** – have your kids sketch the picture that they see straight ahead. This is especially fun if you are driving through a scenic area, like the mountains.
- **Etch-a-sketch or Magna-doodle**
- **Hangman**
- **I spy......**
- **X's and O's**
- **Crossword Puzzles**
- **Word Search**

Maintain School Skills Through Summer

Encourage the kids to keep up their school skills through the summer vacation. It will help them retain what they've already learned and definitely save time reviewing in the fall.

Play Some Games

■ Play a Math Game

With dice

Take a sheet of lined paper and put numbers 1 through 10 in the margin. Using two dice, each player has 10 rolls and the object of the game is to get the highest total. On roll #1, multiply the two dice together and enter the product on the sheet next to the number 1. Continue with the next nine rolls and record each product. After 10 rolls, add up all of the entries to get the grand total. Kids will be motivated to play this game several times and try to get their highest score.

Variations:
- add or subtract the two numbers
- for older kids, construct two dice marked with numbers 7 through 12

# of Rolls	Product
1	12
2	25
3	9
4	6
5	36
6	8
7	15
8	24
9	2
10	10
Total	147

With cards

To begin this math game, remove all the face cards from a deck of cards. Deal the remainder of the cards between two players. Play now begins and is similar to the card game called 'War'. Both players take their top card and turn it over simultaneously. The players quickly multiply the two cards in their head and whoever calls out the correct answer first, wins. The winner takes these two cards and adds them to the bottom of their card pile. The object of the game is to get all of the cards (or the most) within a certain time limit.

Variations:
- use only cards numbered 1 to 5 for young players
- add the cards, instead of multiplying
- leave the face cards in to challenge older players, where the Jack is worth 11, the Queen is 12, and the King is 13

■ Play Board Games

Choose board games that involve spelling, like Scrabble or Boggle.

■ Keep a Journal

Have kids journal throughout the summer, describing activities and highlights.

■ Have a Spelling or Math Bee

Organize a spelling or math bee. Vary the words and math questions for each child, taking their grade level into consideration.

■ Play 'Store' with Younger Kids

Gather items exclusively for a grocery store or make your store into a 'general' department store by adding such things as jewellery, small games or stuffed toys. Put price tags on all the items and then use either pretend money, if you have it available, or real change and bills. Have children take turns being the clerk or the buyer. The clerks can learn how to make change, while the buyers make purchasing decisions. Buyers can also calculate whether or not they received the correct change from the clerk. The kids can have fun figuring how many 75¢ stuffies they can buy for $5.00, or how much change they will receive from $2.00 if their purchase adds up to $1.65. Will they have enough change left over for a 50¢ granola bar? Vary the prices and questions depending on their ages and mathematical ability.

Add an Incentive

In order to keep kids motivated to enhance their school skills over the summer, offer an incentive. Perhaps some concert tickets for the end of the summer or a new backpack for school will help encourage your child and reward them for their effort.

★ *"My son was in grade two and struggling with his spelling. The school year had come to a close and we wanted a strategy to work on over the summer. We devised a plan that involved spelling practice and quizzes. His incentive was a new watch for school, which he picked out, I bought and tucked away. His final goal was to have 75 words spelled correctly out of 80. The timing was great; he ended up taking his final quiz just before we left for our summer vacation in August. He was pretty excited when I presented him with the brand new watch and he was proud of himself too. I personally, felt reassured he was more prepared for grade three."* ★

Foster Summer Reading

Summer is a great time to dive into a good book or to really nurture reading. Create an environment that encourages your children to read and make reading a part of everyday living. When you help your child become a better reader, they will learn more easily and confidently. As their reading improves, so does comprehension, and this benefits all subject areas in school, from math problem solving to difficult science concepts. The benefits in language arts are almost automatic—good readers often become good writers.

Create a Reading Environment

- Have your kids join a 'Reading Club' during the summer.
- Keep a variety of reading material on hand: fiction, non-fiction, poetry, comics, magazines and newspapers.
- Keep reading materials in handy places around the house; by the bed, in the living room, den, bathroom and kitchen.
- Take books along in the car.
- Give books as gifts.
- Visit the public library regularly.
- Spend time at a bookstore, carefully selecting quality books to purchase.
- Model reading – make reading a part of your life; let your child see you *in action.*

★ *"One summer we let our ten and twelve year-olds stay up as late as they wanted, as long as they were reading in bed. It was such a novelty for them to stay up late, that they would both read and read. They went through a lot of books that summer and it certainly helped their reading skills."* ★

Garage sales and second-hand bookstores are a great source for used books at a significantly reduced price.

Be Involved

■ When your child is reading alone:

- Help them to choose books that are at their reading level and definitely not too difficult.
- Be sure to ask them to tell you about their book, for instance, *Was it a good story?*
       Tell me about what happened…

■ When you are reading with your child:

- This is a good time to choose a more challenging book than they would normally read by themselves.
- Share the reading, your child reads one page or section and you read the next.
- Try 'echo reading' for variety. This is where you read at the same time as your child.
- Check for comprehension by asking your child questions.

  How did you like the book?
  What was one of your favourite parts?
  Who was the main character?
  What was the setting?
  Who was the good guy or the protagonist?
  Who was the bad guy or antagonist?
  How did the book make you feel?

■ When your child really enjoys a book:

- Seek out other books by the same author.
- Give your child another book in a similar genre.

■ Organize a 'Share-a-Book' night:

Invite some of your child's friends over and ask them to bring one or two of their favourite books. Have everyone give a brief description of the book(s) they brought and why they enjoyed reading them. Once everyone has had a turn, pass a sheet of paper around and get each person to write

- their name
- the title of their book(s)
- the author(s)
- brief description of the book (optional)

Copy the sheet for all the kids and they'll have a list of some great new books to read.

You may find the kids want to lend out their favourite books to a friend. Write these details on your book list, as well. This will keep track of books that were borrowed and by whom.

Raising Kids...for the fun of it!

Helping a 'Reluctant Reader'

If your child is a "reluctant reader', it may be for one of several reasons. Maybe they've been pushed too hard at some point, or the books they've attempted have been too difficult. Perhaps the stories they've been reading are boring or irrelevant to them. Maybe they cannot deal with distractions while reading, such as TV noise or other family noise in the house. It is possible that your child may not like reading because they do not like to be alone. Some children are so 'social' that they really don't enjoy the solitude when reading by themselves.

There may be a more serious reason that your child has been turned off to reading. Perhaps they have been embarrassed in class when reading out loud. Or possibly they've noticed that their younger siblings or friends read better than they do. Whatever the reason, try to be patient, empathetic and understanding. Here are some ways to support a child that is reluctant about reading.

Strategies to Assist Your Child

- Get help in selecting books for your child. Go to a quality bookstore with knowledgeable staff and ask them for help in selecting a book for your child. Let them know the age, gender and reading level of your child, as well as your child's interests.
- Talk with your child's teacher to see what books they would recommend for them.
- Go to the bookstore and library with your child and help them choose books to read.
- Make sure the reading choices are not too difficult for their reading level.
- Read together and congratulate them when they try a more difficult selection.
- Include fiction and non-fiction books.
- Read the cartoons in the newspaper.
- Subscribe to a magazine for your child.
- Ask other parents what books their children enjoy.
- Ask a librarian for help; perhaps they know of books or resources to assist parents with reluctant readers.
- Try motivating them. Create a reading chart and provide an incentive after a certain number of books, pages or chapters have been read.
- Make reading fun by using a lot of expression when you are reading or even by having some silly props to use during the story.

★ "My son was struggling to learn how to read and was becoming a reluctant reader. We both shed many tears through this whole process. I needed to create an environment that was fun for him to read in. So, we started having 'popcorn parties' in my bed on the weekends. We'd bring stacks of children's books to bed along with a big bowl of popcorn, then cuddle up and read together while munching away. I'd ask him which book he wanted to read the most and that's the one we'd start with. I would begin reading to him and then encourage him to read a bit. Then I'd take another turn reading again. After some time he would get tired, so we'd lie there and discuss the books we had just read. I'd ask which one was his favourite and why, and then I'd tell him which book I liked the most. Afterwards, I would pick up the book I was currently reading and tell him a bit about it. I'd read a little of my book to him and then tell him it was my turn to read to myself. Pretty soon my reluctant reader was picking up one of his books and reading himself to sleep. It's been years now since we've had a popcorn party in my bed. Thankfully, my son is now an avid reader, who reads years above grade level." ★

Raising Kids…for the fun of it!

Family Fun

Camping, Cottage 'n Beach Fun

There's nothing like a day at the beach, a weekend at a cottage or an overnight camping trip to create great family memories. With no TV, computer or electronic games, *family fun* takes on a whole new meaning. Away from adult distractions too, it's a perfect opportunity to really *play* with the kids. Here are some great ways to spend the day, including a variety of activities that are easily organized, inexpensive, and that require very few supplies.

Family Fun at the Beach

■ Build Sand Castles

Gather together plastic containers, pails, shovels, small rakes and take them all to the beach. Have your family work together to build your best sand castle ever. Add a moat surrounding the castle, construct a drawbridge to get across the moat, and add sticks or flags for the turrets.

■ Sand Sculpting

Take a large bed sheet to spread out on the beach. It's cooler than a blanket, easier to clean and lighter to carry.

Try 'sculpting' a whale or a dolphin, an alligator or a mermaid, a turtle, a car or maybe even an airplane out of sand. Sculpting is where you create something out of a big mound of sand. First, use a full-sized spade to shovel the moist sand into a huge pile and pack it down really well. Now, using your hands or small shovels, you can shape your design. Smaller tools such as spoons, sticks or screwdrivers can be used to add detail, such as fins on a mermaid.

Pack sand toys in a mesh bag, so the excess sand can fall out and the contents dry quickly.

★ *"Last summer was the first time I had ever seen sand sculpting. We had no idea what the two guys were doing as they shovelled a huge pile of sand into one spot. They worked on it for hours and designed an incredible lion that we all marvelled over."* ★

■ 'Easy-to-Use' Sporting Equipment

Take along sporting equipment that is easy for everyone to use. Soft nerf footballs are painless to catch. Children prefer soft-sided Frisbees to the hard plastic ones. If you're playing catch with baseball gloves, use a tennis ball rather than a hardball. A medium weight beach ball makes playing volleyball effortless. Play on the sand or in the water. Tackle football is much more fun when you can land in the water. A game takes on a whole new sense of fun when you see how far you can dive to catch the before it hits the water!

> ***Toddler Baseball Set** – Everyone can enjoy a game of baseball with a toddler baseball set. The ball is easy to hit because it is such a large target. The bat is large but lightweight; the weight makes it easy to swing and the size helps kids to contact the ball more easily. It is a great set to use in a confined space such as the beach or the campsite, because the ball doesn't travel very far.*

■ Partner Frisbee Game

Playing catch with a Frisbee on the beach can be fun but how about a Frisbee competition? You play this Frisbee game in teams of two and because it's a fairly easy game, you can choose almost any combination, for example Parents vs. Kids.

Game set up: Position the teams of two approximately 6-10 yds. (5-10 m) apart, depending on throwing ability. Adjust distance if necessary, once you are playing. One player from each team stands slightly ahead of the other, so you clearly have a 'front' player and a 'back' player.

Object of game: To reach 21 points first.

Scoring: To score, both participants in a pair must contact the Frisbee. The person at the front usually touches the Frisbee slightly, trying not to alter the its path and the person at the back attempts to catch it. Either player can throw the Frisbee back to the opposing team so they can attempt to tip and then catch the Frisbee to score.

Raising Kids…for the fun of it!

1 point – if the person at the front touches the Frisbee with their finger or hand, and the back person catches it.
2 points – if the front person touches it with their foot and the back person catches it.
2 points – if the front person touches it and the second person catches it behind their back.
3 points – if there are three alternating contacts, specifically the front player tips Frisbee slightly, the back player tips it back to front person and they catch it.

Note: Reverse the order of your team after awhile. The front person goes to the back and takes a turn at catching, the back person moves to the front where their job is to 'tip' the Frisbee.

★ *"We were camping with another family and the Moms challenged the teenage boys to a Frisbee competition. The boys got right into it; you'd see them giving each other high fives after working together to make a difficult or diving catch. The Moms too, were laughing and cheering each other on. We had quite a few spectators after a while; people really enjoyed watching the game. It ended with a close score and it was big fun! The best part was that the next day it was the teenagers who requested a rematch against the Moms."* ★

Variation:
'Partner Frisbee' With More Than Two Teams
If there are three teams of two players, just form a triangle between teams. If there are four teams, rather than have so much wait-time between turns, split into two separate games going on simultaneously, with a Frisbee for each game. The team that reaches 21 points first is the overall winner.

Alternately, you could have a small tournament. The winners of the first round would playoff for the 'championship title'. The two teams who lost the first round could playoff against each other for the 'consolation title'.

Meanwhile...Back at the Campsite

Once you're back at the campsite for the day, there are many possibilities for things to do. Some activities can be done by the kids alone, where they use their imagination and their own resources. But other ideas the parents will be anxious to try too, right along with the kids.

■ Check out the Interpretive Centres

Check out the campground's interpretive centre, you may be pleasantly surprised by the variety and number of programs readily available. Some interpretive centres have hikes or nature walks, crafts for the kids or even Karaoke.

■ Create a 'Kid's Kamp'

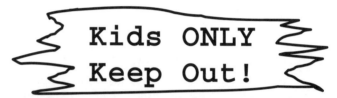

Kids ONLY Keep Out!

Gather tarps, pup tents, hammocks, lawn chairs and small tables together. Let the kids construct an area designated *'For Kids Only'*. Begin by using tarps and tarp straps to section off an area of your campsite and then let them design a space all to themselves.

★ *"Our Kid's Kamp idea developed and grew through the years. It started long ago when we were camping with two very special families. The Dads decided to section off an area that gave the three families a bit of privacy. The weather was rotten so they put tarps overhead, as well. Pretty soon the kids asked to have an area to themselves and the 'Kamp' idea began. Over time, the kids added hammocks for relaxing and reading on, tables for doing crafts or playing cards together and pup tents to play in. Each year they'd add more features. Often you would see signs outside their area with 'Private—Keep out!' or 'Kids ONLY' written upon it. It was fun to watch the kids design their own space. They loved having an area to 'hang out' and have all to themselves. An unexpected bonus was that the parents got a bit of peace and quiet too, which was quite a treat especially when the kids were young."* ★

Raising Kids...for the fun of it!

■ Whittle a Walking Stick

While away your time by the campfire and give whittling a try. Be sure the kids are old enough to be steady with their hands and strong enough to actually 'whittle' a piece of wood. Close parental guidance will be needed at first. When they are capable and ready, it's a great way to spend time relaxing at the campsite. It's also nice to take home a memento they've made on the trip.

★ *"Whittling has become a family favourite while camping. Our boys carved their first walking stick with a small jack knife. One year we took the walking sticks home and varnished them. We placed each of them in a vice grip and hammered a large copper coupling on to the bottom. We've even talked of hanging a 'bear bell' from the end. Our kids enjoyed whittling so much; we purchased a wood carving set that we take along on all of our camping trips."* ★

■ Construct an 'Outdoor Germ-Buster'

Take 'germ-buster' materials along on your summer get-away and follow the steps below to construct one. Once it's made, you won't have to talk the kids into washing up. Hang it up outside your cottage or close to your picnic table at the campsite and you'll always have soap and water handy.

What you'll do:
1. Using a nail, puncture the bottom corner (corner opposite the handle) of the milk jug, making a small hole.
2. Tie one end of the string to the handle of the milk jug and the other end of the string to the golf tee.
3. Use the golf tee to plug the hole made by the nail and fill the milk jug with water.
4. Place the bar of soap in one leg of the panty hose and attach it securely to the handle of the jug.
5. Loop the remaining leg of the panty hose through the top part of the handle and secure it. Now use the rest of the hosiery to tie the *germ-buster* to a tree or picnic table.
6. When it's time to wash up, just pop out the golf tee and you have *running water*. Plug the hole once your hands are wet and use the bar of soap to lather up. Pull out the tee once again to rinse your hands clean.

What you'll need:
- 4-litre plastic milk jug – washed and rinsed
- nail
- golf tee
- 24" (60 cm) piece of string
- pair of panty hose
- bar of soap

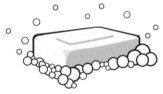

★ *"My kids' hands were never so clean as the weekend we hung our germ-buster by the campfire. The girls 'washed up' before every meal and snack and then washed up some more times in between. It was fun to make and what a novelty to have."* ★

■ Go on a Scavenger Hunt

Create a list of items for the kids to find, such as a red rock, feather, live bug, pine needle, a stem with opposite leaves (across from one another), a stem with alternating leaves, bark, straw and an empty pop can. Set the boundaries for the hunt and let the game begin. If you have a lot of kids or young ones that need supervision, let them go 'hunting' in pairs. When the search is complete, be sure to examine all their wonderful finds. Reward all eager hunters with a small treat or snack.

★ *"Once I send the kids out on a scavenger hunt, I often look around for other items of interest. The hunting is so much fun, chances are they'll want to go out on another one, shortly after they return. I'm happy to be all ready with another list."* ★

Family Fun

Family Card Games

Pull out the cards and teach your kids some of these old favourites. Included are the rules for two great games, 'Spoons' and 'Speed'. These two card games are suitable for multi-ages, making them perfect for families. Check out the library or internet for the other card game rules.

• War	• Speed
• Rummy	• Crib
• Uno	• Spoons
• 7-Step Rummy	• Double Series/Sequence
• Crazy Eights	• Double Solitaire
• Old Maid	• 31

★ *"I love to watch families playing cards at a campsite. The best part is watching the different ages interact, like Grandpa playing crib with a teenager, or Mom challenging a preschooler to a game of Crazy Eights. Cards are a great activity to connect across the generations."* ★

Spoons

Number of players: 3 or more

Materials:
- 1 deck of cards
- spoons, one per participant
- 3 tokens for each player, such as toothpicks or pennies
- small container to hold the tokens

Object of the game: To get two pairs or four of a kind in your hand and then pick up your spoon.

Game set-up: Place one spoon per player in the middle of the table. Give each player three tokens and put the empty container in the middle, as well. Deal each player four cards that they secretly look at but leave face down on the table in front of them. The dealer keeps the remainder of the cards in a separate pile, called the 'playing pile', face-down beside him.

The play: The dealer signals the beginning of the play by saying, '1-2-3-Go'. Everyone passes one card to the player on their right. All players (except the dealer) pick up the card that has been passed to them. The dealer however, picks one card from the playing pile. All players look at their new card to see if it matches any that they have in their hand. If it does, they keep that card in their hand, which gives them a matching pair.

On the next signal 'go', everyone passes another card that does not match in their hand to the right. Continue in this manner ('go' and pass, 'go' and pass), passing unwanted cards to the right, until someone gets two pairs or four of a kind. When this happens, the person secretly or discretely grabs a spoon. They quietly stop playing because they have the cards they need and therefore do not want to pass any more cards. As the other players realize that one person has grabbed a spoon, they quickly grab one too. The last person to grab a spoon loses the round. When you lose a round, you must put one of your tokens in the container. When players have lost four times they are out of the game. This includes losing their three tokens in three different rounds plus losing one extra round, called their 'free round'.

The winner: The winner is determined by continuing to play until all but one player has lost their three tokens and has also lost their free round. The single remaining player is the winner.

> ★ *"We played Spoons at band camp with adults and teenagers. Players were literally jumping across the table to grab a spoon—we laughed so hard that our stomachs were sore."* ★

Speed

Number of players: 2

Materials: 2 decks of cards

Object of the game: To be the first person to lay down all the cards in your hand and all the cards in your pick-up pile.

Game set-up: Deal four piles face down, two piles of cards for each player, one pile of seven cards for their hand and one pile of thirteen cards designated as their *pick-up pile*. Split the remainder of the cards evenly into two piles. No need to deal these, but simply estimate two equal piles, and lay them face down, as well. These two piles are called the 'playing piles' and both are placed in the centre of the table, with ample space between them (see diagram).

Diagram:

Player #1's Side

The Hand   The Pick-up Pile

| 7 | | 13 |

★ *"Play this card game if you really want to get the adrenaline flowing—it is very fast-paced."* ★

Player #1
Playing Pile

Player # 2
Playing Pile

| 7 | | 13 |

The Hand   The Pick-up Pile

Player #2's Side

The play: To start the play, both players will simultaneously say 'ready-set-go'. Each player then turns over the top card of their playing pile and puts it face-up in the middle or the dotted areas (see diagram). This begins the game and both players may now lay the cards from their hand on either turned up card. A card can only be played when:

- it is one number higher or lower than the last card played on either pile.
- and it alternates in colour, red-black-red-black, etc.

Examples:
- red 6 on dotted pile – play either a black 5 or 7
- black King on dotted pile – play either a red Queen or a red Ace

Once you lay a card from your hand down on either dotted pile, you quickly replace it with one from your pick-up pile, to ensure that you always have seven cards in your hand.

Note: *Often the play stops because neither player has any cards in their hand that can be laid on the playing pile. At this point, both players count out loud, '1-2-3' and then each turn over a fresh, new card from their playing pile onto the centre piles, face-up. This will usually restart the play—but if not, repeat again.*

The winner: The first player to lay down all the cards in their hand *and* their pick-up pile, and then say '*Speed*' is the winner.

Raising Kids…for the fun of it!

Campfire Activities

The campfire is the perfect location for some more fun and games. Check out the song-singing and the story-telling.

Silly Songs

The following is a list of good campfire songs. They are easy to sing and will get a lot of laughs too. The words are provided for the songs marked with a diamond (♦).

Songs to create lines for:
Hey Laudie ♦
Down By The Bay ♦

Action songs:
My Bonnie Lies Over the Ocean ♦
Head & Shoulders, Knees & Toes
B.I.N.G.O. ♦

A song to challenge your memory:
Hole in the Bottom of The Sea ♦

Fun repeating after the leader:
The Other Day I Met a Bear ♦

A tongue twister:
Glory, Glory How Peculiar

Songs sung in rounds:
Row, Row, Row Your Boat
Frere' Jacques

A song to sing softly and go louder:
John Jacob Jingleheimer Smith

> Jazz up the songs by using some creative musical instruments:
> • spoons to bang together
> • pots as drums
> • containers filled with popcorn or rocks for tambourines
> Stand up when it's your turn to sing, do the actions—just let loose!

★ *"We were camping one summer and came across an old songbook in our motor home. I started telling the kids about some songs we used to sing and how we'd make up the lines in the rhyming ones. It wasn't long before we were all singing, shouting out silly, made-up rhymes and having a riot. Now we take that songbook on vacation wherever we go."* ★

■ 'Hey Laudie'

Go through the entire group of people at the campfire and make up a verse about each one. Everyone sings the chorus in between verses which allows enough time for someone to make up a rhyme about the next person. There are a few examples listed below.

Begin with the chorus:
Hey laudie, laudie, laudie
Hey laudie, laudie, lo.
Hey laudie, laudie, laudie
Hey laudie, laudie, lo.

Verse #1:
There are no verses to this song,
Hey laudie, laudie, lo.
You just make them up as you go along,
Hey laudie, laudie, lo.

Chorus

I know a gal who's name is Heather,
Hey laudie, laudie, lo.
She is as light as a feather,
Hey laudie, laudie, lo.

Chorus

I know a guy who's name is Bert,
Hey laudie, laudie, lo.
He sure likes to be a flirt,
Hey laudie, laudie, lo.

If you can't find a word that rhymes with their name, put their name in the middle of the sentence or just point to the person that you are referring to.

I know Asha who's full of fun, (name in the middle)
Hey laudie, laudie, lo.
But when she starts to sing, we all run.
Hey laudie, laudie, lo.

I know a guy who's kinda cute, (point to the guy)
Hey laudie, laudie, lo.
But when he eats beans, he likes to toot.
Hey laudie, laudie, lo.

Raising Kids…for the fun of it!

■ 'Down by the Bay'

This song is done in two groups, with the first group singing the initial line and then the second group repeating it. Half the fun is in repeating the lines and the other half is in making up the rhymes.

> *Down by the bay......down by the bay,*
>   (first group)   (second group)
> *Where the watermelons grow......where the watermelons grow,*
> *Back to my home.......back to my home,*
> *I dare not go..........I dare not go.*
> *For if I do......for if I do,*
> *My mother would say......my mother would say,*
> *Did you ever see a cow with a green eyebrow?*
> *Down by the bay.*
>
> Repeat it all again, but change the question in each verse:
>   *Did you ever see a bee with a sunburnt knee?*
>   *Did you ever see a bear in his underwear?*
>   *Did you ever see a swan with a bow tie on?*
>   *Did you ever see a moose kissing a goose?*
>   (And make up the rest!)

■ 'My Bonnie Lies Over the Ocean'

Try this one while everyone is sitting around the campfire in a group. On the first word of the song that starts with the letter 'B', everyone must get up and stay standing while they sing. On the next word that starts with 'B' they must sit down and remain sitting until the next B-word. It's a riot to see who has followed all the directions carefully and is actually sitting by the end.

> *My **B**onnie lies over the ocean,*
>   *(stand up)*
> *My **B**onnie lies over the sea,*
>   *(sit down)*
> *My **B**onnie lies over the ocean,*
>   *(up)*
> *Oh **b**ring **b**ack my **B**onnie to me.*
>   *(down) (up)   (down)*
>
> ***Bring back, bring back,***
>   *(up) (down) (up) (down)*
> *Oh **b**ring **b**ack my **B**onnie to me, to me.*
>   *(up) (down)   (up)*
> ***Bring back, bring back,***
>   *(down) (up) (down) (up)*
> *Oh **b**ring **b**ack my **B**onnie to me.*
>   *(down) (up)   (down)*

■ 'B.I.N.G.O.'

Try out your co-ordination and rhythm with this song.

1. *There was a farmer had a dog and Bingo was his name-O.*
   (Spell it out 3 times)   *B-I-N-G-O*
                                 B-I-N-G-O
                                 B-I-N-G-O
                                 And Bingo was his name-O!

2. *There was a farmer had a dog and Bingo was his name-O.*
   (Clap for the B)   *clap-I-N-G-O*
                                 clap-I-N-G-O
                                 clap-I-N-G-O
                                 And Bingo was his name-O!

3. Repeat, clapping for B and I.   *clap-clap-N-G-O*
4. Repeat, clapping for B, I, and N.   *clap-clap-clap-G-O*
5. Repeat, clapping for B, I, N, and G.   *clap-clap-clap-clap-O*
6. Repeat, clapping for all the letters.   *clap-clap-clap-clap-clap*
                                            and *Bingo was his name-O!*

■ 'Hole in the Bottom of the Sea'

This particular song is one that can really drive you crazy. Challenge your mind, your memory, and your patience!

There's a hole in the bottom of the sea.
There's a hole in the bottom of the sea.
There's a hole, there's a hole,
There's a hole, there's a hole,
There's a hole in the bottom of the sea.

There's a log in the hole in the bottom of the sea.
There's a log in the hole in the bottom of the sea.
There's a log, there's a log,
There's a log, there's a log,
There's a log in the hole in the bottom of the sea.

There's a bump on the log in the hole in the bottom of the sea, etc.

There's a frog on the bump on the log in the hole in the bottom of the sea, etc.

There's a wart............flea..........hair............germ.

Here's an example of the entire song completed (or make up your own version):
There's a germ on the hair on the flea on the wart on the frog on the bump on the log in the hole in the bottom of the sea.

Raising Kids…for the fun of it!

■ 'The Other Day I Met a Bear'

For this particular song you sing each verse through twice. The first time you will sing it in two parts, one group or person sings the first phrase, the second group or person sings the phrase again (see brackets). After a verse is sung in this manner, the whole verse is sung again without repeats, where both groups are singing it all together. It is a great song that's a lot of fun!

The other day (the other day), I met a bear (I met a bear),
    group 1   group 2   group 1   group 2
Up in the woods (up in the woods), a way up there (a way up there).
    group 1   group 2   group 1   group2
The other day I met a bear, up in the woods, a way up there.
    all together

He looked at me (he looked at me), I looked at him (I looked at him),
He sized me up (he sized me up), I sized up him (I sized up him).
He looked at me, I looked at him, he sized me up, I sized up him.

He said to me (he said to me), why don't you run (why don't you run),
I see you ain't (I see you ain't), got any gun (got any gun).
He said to me, why don't you run? I see you ain't got any gun.

And so I ran (and so I ran), away from there (away from there),
But right behind (but right behind), me was that bear (me was that bear).
And so I ran away from there, but right behind me was that bear.

Continue in the same pattern for the rest of the verses:

Ahead of me, I saw a tree,
A great big tree, ahead of me.

The nearest branch, was ten feet up,
I'd have to jump, and trust my luck.

And so I jumped, into the air,
But I missed that branch, away up there.

Now don't you fret, and don't you frown,
Cause I caught that branch, on the way back down.

That's all there is, there ain't no more,
Unless I meet, that bear once more.

Storytelling Around the Campfire

The perfect place for storytelling is around the campfire. As the logs are crackling and the flames are shooting high, use the following questions to really get the stories flowing.

■ Personal Stories

- *What was one of your most embarrassing moments?*
- *Tell me about a time that you were really scared.*
- *What is one of the strangest or funniest things a teacher ever said in class, or that a teacher ever did in class?*
- *What is the funniest thing a classmate has ever said to a teacher?*
- *What is the one of the best gifts you ever received?*

■ Hypothetical questions

- *What would you do with a million dollars?*
- *If you could be any famous person, who would you be and why?*
- *If you could be any animal, what would you be?*
- *Which famous athlete would you like to be and why?*
- *What do you want to be when you grow up?*

> ★ *"I'll never forget the story Mom told us about her grade six teacher. She had her class playing volleyball in the gym and she accidentally got hit in the head by the ball. Her wig flew off and landed about three feet away. The kids didn't know what to do so they started to laugh. She started laughing too as she scrambled over to pick her wig up off the floor. This was such a great teacher's story, everyone at the campfire was now anxious to tell a silly story of their own."* ★

■ Storytelling

Older kids enjoy telling scary stories; have them make one up as they go along. Or have a book of short frightening stories on hand to take turns reading from.

> ★ *"Our favourite night activity is lighting bulrush torches. During the day, we find a pond or slough where the bulrush plants or 'cat tails' grow and we each select a few. After we're back at the cabin, my husband dips them in citronella oil. The kids light the ends by holding them over the campfire flame. We carry the torches all around the yard, one year we pretended we were at the Olympics passing the big Olympic torch. Some times we march with the torches held high or often we do dance moves. When we have friends out to the lake, they tell us it was the highlight of their trip."* ★

Raising Kids…for the fun of it!

Raising Kids…for the fun of it!

Raising Kids…for the fun of it!

Raising Kids…for the fun of it!

About the Authors

L-R Gloria McInnis, Wendy Johnson, Heather Tansem
Photo by Flo Slomp, FJS Inc.

Gloria, Wendy and Heather approach life with energy and enthusiasm. Professionally, they are dedicated and resourceful—Wendy with her work in the technology department at Edmonton Public Schools, Gloria with her focus on marketing and sales, and Heather while she worked as a teacher at Leduc Jr. High. Work was done with purpose and innovation. It was not a surprise then, when parenthood came their way, they approached it with the same passion and commitment.

While their kids were young, they joined a Mom's group that met one morning a week. It was always a time for visiting and connecting. Challenges were discussed, ideas were shared, problems were solved and triumphs were celebrated. As a group, they constantly recognized the value of sharing ideas and helping each other during this phase of parenting. So many great ideas were discussed; you'd often hear as part of the conversation, *'We ought to write a book!'* And so, it all began... In the initial stages of the book, there were three other special friends involved that the authors would like to acknowledge: Linda Grisley, Brenda Mitchke, and Jeanne Raikles.

The sharing has continued as their kids have gone from playschool to elementary, and onto junior and senior high. Throughout this time, Gloria, Wendy and Heather have focused their creative energy on *Raising Kids...for the fun of it!*

★ *"Initially, when my kids were small, I joined 'Mom's Morning Out' so they could get together with other kids their own age. But, I stayed with the group for my own benefit—it grew to be an important support system."* ★

Contact Information

To order additional copies, book a speaker, or share an idea from your family—please contact the authors either by:

Mail
Raising Kids
P.O. Box 45087,
Lansdowne Postal Outlet,
Edmonton, Alberta,
Canada T6H 5Y1

Email authors@raisingkids.ca

Website www.raisingkids.ca

The perfect gift or resource for:
- ☑ Parents
- ☑ Grandparents
- ☑ Aunts & Uncles
- ☑ Teachers

- ☑ Day Care Providers
- ☑ Home Schoolers
- ☑ Youth Directors
- ☑ Camp Counselors

- ☑ Anyone who deals with kids

"This book gives parents concrete examples and realistic suggestions for family routines that respect children's needs while helping parents keep their sanity. A must read for today's parent!"

Helena Beça, Early Childhood Educator
Edmonton Preschool Association, President

Raising Kids…for the fun of it!